SS

D1201359

1
RAILROAD CAPITALIZATION

STUDIES IN HISTORY, ECONOMICS AND PUBLIC LAW

EDITED BY THE FACULTY OF POLITICAL SCIENCE OF
COLUMBIA UNIVERSITY

Volume XCV]   [Number 1

Whole Number 215

RAILROAD CAPITALIZATION

A Study of the Principles of Regulation
of Railroad Securities

BY

JAMES C. BONBRIGHT

AMS PRESS
NEW YORK

COLUMBIA UNIVERSITY
STUDIES IN THE
SOCIAL SCIENCES

215

The Series was formerly known as
Studies in History, Economics and Public Law.

Reprinted with the permission of Columbia University Press
From the edition of 1920, New York
First AMS EDITION published 1969
Manufactured in the United States of America

H
31
.C7
#215
1969

Library of Congress Catalogue Card Number: 70-78003

AMS PRESS, INC.
NEW YORK, N. Y. 10003

PREFACE

When Congress included in the Transportation Act of 1920 a provision giving to the Interstate Commerce Commission full and exclusive control over the issue of securities by interstate carriers, it brought to a close one of the sharpest and most protracted controversies that have been waged in the field of railroad regulation. This controversy was concerned with the question of the public interest in railroad capitalization. For years, stock watering has been attacked in and out of Congress as one of the most vicious practices of private railway managements; for years, popular discussions have held it responsible for exorbitant rates and inefficient service. Yet, until recently, railway officials have insisted that neither stock watering nor any other form of overcapitalization is a matter of public concern; and, until recently, their views have prevailed with the lawmakers, to the extent, at least, of preventing public control. Now all this is changed. First the states, and at last the federal government have seen the necessity of financial control as a means of securing reasonable rates and adequate service.

But though the principle of public control is now a settled issue, the problems connected with this control are by no means settled. Railways, we say, should be properly capitalized. But what is proper capitalization? And how is it to be secured under government control? These are questions on which Congress and the Interstate Commerce Commission will have to spend much thought and effort. Success or failure in finding the correct answers will be one of the deciding factors in the larger issue of private *versus* government ownership.

The present work is a study of some of these problems. It makes no attempt to cover the entire subject of security regulation—a subject almost as intricate and comprehensive as the kindred subject of rate regulation—but confines itself to the more fundamental principles and the more important issues. Special attention is given to the problem of stock watering. Stock watering is an evil for which three very different remedies have been proposed. The first remedy is to prevent the practice by requiring that no shares be issued at less than their par value; the second is to allow stock watering to continue, but to render it harmless by giving full publicity to the actual investment; the third is to meet the problem by issuing shares of stock without par value. Or, to put it in other words, the first measure would make the par values indicate the true investment; the second would expose the par values as a pure fiction; the third would abolish par values entirely. Each of these three methods has won the support of eminent authority; each has been put into practice by various state governments. Which of the three should be adopted by the federal government is a problem discussed at length in the present study.

For a brief review of the points developed in this study, the reader is referred to the summary or conclusion at the end of each chapter. Chapter I analyzes the effect of capitalization on the rate level and on the quality of the service. An extended discussion of the relation between capitalization and rates seemed to be called for, not merely because of the wide differences of opinion which have hitherto prevailed on the subject, but also because of the practical bearing of this problem on the objects and methods of security regulation. The conclusion of the first chapter is that capitalization influences rates and services primarily through its effect on railway credit. Chapter II, therefore, considers precisely how capitalization may influence the corporate credit—to what extent overcapitalization weakens the financial structure. A discussion of the evil effects of overcapitalization naturally raises the question, What is proper capitalization? In Chapter III this problem is treated under the heading, " the Basis of Capitalization." A study of the experience of the various state commissions leads to the conclusion that the whole attempt to make capitalization correspond to the corporate assets is impracticable, and that it should be abandoned in favor of the plan of issuing shares of stock without par value. Chapter IV considers in detail this recent financial device and defends it against current criticisms. A concluding chapter is devoted to a discussion of three of the special problems connected with the federal regulation of railway securities.

The material for this study is drawn largely from the reports of decisions rendered by the various state public service commissions on the applications of public utility companies for permission to issue securities. State commissions are the pioneers in the field of security regulation, and their experience will serve as a guide to the federal government. In most states, control over security issues extends both to railways and to local public utilities, but the general principles involved are identical despite some differences in detail. Therefore, although the present treatise is written with special reference to the problem of the railways, the writer has not hesitated to cite as precedents decisions with respect to public utilities of all classes. In these citations, the abbreviation " P. U. R." refers to the *Public Utilities Reports, Annotated* (Rochester, N. Y., Lawyers Cooperative Publishing Company, 1915-   ).

Among the unofficial literature on the subject, the author owes much to the writings of Barron, Heilman, Ignatius, and Ripley. The last named author's work on *Railroads, Finance and Organization* has been a constant and valued companion in the preparation of this study. More specific references to the writings of these and other authors are given in the footnotes and in the bibliography at the end.

Several specialists have been kind enough to read parts of the manuscript. For this service the author is much indebted to Dr. John Bauer, and to Professors Henry R. Hatfield, Roy B. Kester, Hastings Lyon, T. W. Van Metre, and Allyn A. Young. Each of these men has made valued suggestions and criticisms resulting in the modification of manuscript. The study as a whole has been made under the direction of Professor Seligman. To him, most of all, the writer would express his deep gratitude for constant help and stimulating guidance.

COLUMBIA UNIVERSITY, JUNE, 1920.

TABLE OF CONTENTS

CHAPTER I

THE EFFECT OF CAPITALIZATION ON RAILWAY RATES AND SERVICE

GOVERNMENTAL control of railroad securities is favored as a necessary protection both to the investor and to the public. Obviously, however, the public interest is paramount, and the discussion in this treatise is entirely from that point of view. What the public demands of the railways is the best possible service at the lowest possible rates. Its chief concern in the regulation of railway securities must lie, therefore, in the possible effect of capitalization on rates and on service.

Very unfortunate has been the tendency in public discussion of railroad problems to emphasize the problem of rates to the exclusion of the problem of service. With respect to capitalization this tendency is particularly to be deplored, for the financial structure of railway corporations has a much more decided influence upon the quality of the service than upon the rate level.[1] Too often, this more serious charge against overcapitalization has been neglected in a vain attempt to prove a closer relation than really exists between securities and rates. It is nevertheless true that capitalization does have some effect on rates as well as on service. We therefore divide this chapter into two parts,

[1] S. O. Dunn, *Regulation of Railways* (New York, 1918), p. 136; W. Z. Ripley, *Railroads, Finance and Organization* (New York, 1915), p. 282.

the first part discussing the problem of rates, and the second
part discussing the problem of service.

1. EFFECT OF CAPITALIZATION ON RATES

No railway problem has given rise to more dispute, or to
greater extremes of opinion, than the question of the relation between the amount of outstanding securities and the
transportation charges.[1] While public opinion has always
held stock watering responsible for exorbitant charges, railway officials have constantly denied that capitalization has
any effect whatever on rate schedules. As early as 1874,
the opposing views were clearly set forth in the report of the
" Windom Committee " of the United States Senate.[2] Of
all the abuses with which the railways were charged, " none,"
said the committee, " have contributed so much to the
general discontent and indignation as the increase of railway capital by ' *stockwatering*,' and *capitalization of surplus earnings*. . . . Your committee are of the opinion that

[1] References on the relation between capitalization and rates:
" Windom Committee," *Report*, 1874, 43d Cong., 1st Sess., Sen. Rep.
307, two pts., pt. ii, p. 142, *et seq.*; U. S. Industrial Commission, *Hear-
ings* (1900-1902), vols. iv and ix, Index *s. v.* " Capitalization," also
Report of the Commission, vol. xix, pp. 405, 618; U. S. Congress, House
of Representatives, Committee on Interstate and Foreign Commerce,
*Hearings, February 9 to March 17, 1914, on " Regulation of the Issuance
of Stocks and Bonds by Common Carriers"*; Interstate Commerce
Commission, *Twenty-second Annual Report*, 1908, p. 86; A. T. Hadley,
Railroad Transportation (New York, 1885), pp. 122-24; James F.
Hudson, *The Railways and the Republic* (New York, 1886), ch. vii;
John M. Eshleman, in *Annals of the American Academy of Political
and Social Science*, vol. liii (1914), pp. 148-61; National Association
of Railway Commissioners, *Proceedings of Twenty-ninth Annual Convention*, 1913, pp. 115-223, 238-57; *Journal of Accountancy*, vol. iv
(1907), pp. 327-49, " Railroad Overcapitalization, A Symposium"; E.
S. Mead, *Corporation Finance* (New York, 1915), pp. 147-58; M. B.
Ignatius, *The Financing of Public Service Corporations* (New York,
1918), pp. 267-68, 320-23.

[2] *Op. cit.*

stock inflation is wholly indefensible; that it necessarily produces increased charges, and promotes corrupt speculation, and hence should be prohibited." [1] But the justice of this view was vigorously challenged by spokesmen for the railways who testified before the committee. According to one of them, Mr. Edwin P. Worcester of the New York Central Railway, " there never was such a thing heard of as a company that increased its capital stock as an excuse or occasion for putting up rates. It could just as well put up rates if the business would bear it without increasing the capital, and, if able, pay double the rate of dividend." [2]

The same conflict of opinions has continued down to the present day.[3] It found strong expression in the testimony before the Railroad Securities Committee in 1910. A statement by Judge Lovett before that committee is typical of the railway point of view. " I feel entirely warranted,"

[1] *Op. cit.*, pt. i, pp. 72, 76.

[2] *Ibid.*, pt. i, p. 74.

[3] Although the general position of railway representatives has been as above indicated, there have been one or two exceptions. It would indeed be difficult to find more caustic arraignments of the practice of stock watering than have come from the pen of a railroad president, Mr. Charles Francis Adams, and of a banker, Mr. Henry Clews. The latter, referring to the prevalent custom of issuing large stock bonuses to railroad construction companies, remarked: " It is no exaggeration to characterize these transactions as direct frauds upon the public . . . they are essentially deceptive and unjust, and involve an oppressive taxation of the public at large for the benefit of a few individuals, who have given no equivalent for what they get" (*Fifty Years in Wall Street* [New York, 1908], p. 245). *Cf.* also Adams, " Railroad Inflation," *North American Review*, vol. cviii (1869), pp. 130-64. Very different from the position of Mr. Adams was that of his predecessor and successor as president of the Union Pacific Railway, Mr. Sidney Dillon, who wrote that " as a matter of reason and principle, the question of capitalization concerns the stockholders and the stockholders only. A citizen, simply as a citizen, commits an impertinence when he questions the right of any corporation to capitalize its properties at any sum whatever" (*North American Review*, vol. clii [1891], p. 446).

he said, " in stating that the railroad rates, both passenger
and freight, prevailing throughout the United States today were not made, and were not in any wise influenced, by
the bonds and stocks outstanding, and that the needs of the
companies for interest on bonds and dividends on stock
had nothing whatever to do with the fixing of the rates." [1]

That these opposing views should have been held in the
early days of our experience with railway problems is not
to be wondered at; but that the divergence should have re-
mained as wide as ever after half a century of railway history is indeed surprising.   Perhaps the following study
of the merits of the controversy may throw some light on
the failure to reconcile the differences.

Transportation rates are usually determined, in the first
instance, by the railway management; but they are subject
to approval or revision by government, either through legislation or, more frequently, by order of a regulating commission.   In our study of the effect of capitalization on
rates we must look, then, on the one hand to the voluntary
rate policy of the railway management and, on the other
hand, to the principles of rate control by the government.
Let us consider these two problems in turn.

A. INFLUENCE OF CAPITALIZATION ON A COMPANY'S OWN RATE POLICY

It is often assumed in popular discussions that railways
and public utilities fix such rates as will enable them to earn
interest and dividends on outstanding securities.   From this
it would follow, of course, that an excessive issue of stocks
or bonds would result in excessive rates.   Obviously, however, this assumption is fallacious; corporations are neither
able nor willing to adjust their charges on any such basis.
Their attempt is to secure a maximum profit, whether that

---

[1] *Statement of R. S. Lovett Before the Railroad Securities Commission, December 21, 1910* (New York, 1910?).

be two per cent or twenty per cent on the stock. Charges are limited, either to the rates on competitive lines, or to so-called " monopoly price," based on the principle of " charging what the traffic will bear." A railway might double its capitalization, but it could not thereby stop competition nor increase the capacity of the traffic to bear higher rates. Rates, therefore, except for one qualification about to be mentioned, would remain the same. This fact has long been recognized by railway authorities; it was pointed out at the hearings of the Windom Committee in 1874, and by Hadley in 1885.[1] The wonder is that a fallacy so obvious as is contained in the contrary notion can have persisted to the present.

This conclusion, that increased capitalization would not cause a railway management to raise the rates, is subject to one qualification, a qualification also long ago pointed out by Hadley.[2] When a company is so overcapitalized that

[1] *Railroad Transportation*, pp. 122-4. See also an article by the same author on " Railway Abuses at Home and Abroad," *New Princeton Review*, November, 1886. An excellent recent statement of this principle is given by Edward S. Mead, *Corporation Finance* (New York, 1915), pp. 147-58.

[2] *Railroad Transportation*, pp. 122-24. In theory there is another qualification; namely, that capitalization may affect rates by influencing the amount of construction of competitive railways, thus increasing or decreasing the opportunities to charge monopoly prices. Strangely enough, writers have taken opposite views as to the effect of over-capitalization on competition. Some have held that it tends to stimulate competition by making the overweighted company less strong and formidable as a commercial fighter (Mead, *op. cit.*, p. 149; Clews, *op. cit.*, p. 247). Others have contended that the concealment of profits by means of stock watering tends to deter possible competitors. Of these two positions, the latter is the more plausible. It is strengthened by a further consideration; that overcapitalization, by contributing to railway failures, may discourage investments in railways and so may check competition. But from a practical point of view, the effect of overcapitalization on rates through its influence on competition is so indirect and problematical as to be hardly worth considering.

it finds difficulty in earning the expected rates of interest and dividend, it may resort to a short-sighted policy of rate making in order to secure the earnings required for the immediate future. Where a financially strong company might decide to reduce rates, hoping to be recompensed by gradual increase in traffic, a weak company would be unwilling to risk even a temporary decline in earnings for the sake of an ultimate gain. Conversely, where a prosperous railway would hesitate to raise rates for fear of injury in the long run to its traffic, the impecunious road would stop at nothing that might bring a temporary increase in its earnings. Perhaps one may state the point formally in this way: *The policy of any corporate monopoly with respect to charges (and services) is dictated by two considerations— first, by the desire to make maximum profits in the long run; second, by the desire to avoid even a temporary fall in profits below a certain minimum. Sometimes these two considerations conflict; and when they do conflict, the first usually predominates with financially strong companies,[1] the second predominates with financially weak companies.*

With local public utilities this influence of a company's financial position on its rate policy is sometimes an important factor. Conservatively capitalized, prosperous electric light companies, for example, have not infrequently reduced their rates below the maxima fixed by the regulating commissions, simply in order to build up business and to establish a good-will on the part of the public. But with the interstate railroads it is doubtful whether the principle has been to any considerable degree operative. Railroads are only to a limited extent monopolies; often they have been highly competitive. Competition has usually prevented a weak

---

[1] Not always, however; the controlling interests in a financially sound company sometimes adopt the short-sighted policy in order to sell out at top prices.

or bankrupt road from raising its rates. Some authorities have presented evidence tending to show that rates on over-capitalized railroads have been even lower than on the more conservatively financed lines.[1] The Alton, for example, underwent an upward revision of its capitalization at the beginning of the present century; but in spite of this increase, transportation rates declined materially. A similar situation prevailed on the Rock Island. One of the most excessively capitalized roads in the country is the Chicago Great Western Railway; yet its charges have been among the very lowest. The grossly overcapitalized Erie has charged lower average freight rates per ton-mile than the undercapitalized Lackawanna. Other similar instances might be cited.

Whether these cases really indicate an inverse correlation between capitalization and rates, or whether they are purely a matter of chance, could be proved, if at all, only by more careful statistical studies than have yet been made. Probably the latter explanation is correct; for it so happens that most of the overcapitalized railways that have been cited as charging low rates are located in unusually competitive territory. In theory, however, an actual relation of cause and effect is not out of the question. The very reasons that may induce an overcapitalized *monopolistic* railway to raise its rates may cause an overcapitalized *competitive* railway to lower them. In both cases the short-sighted desire to secure maximum immediate returns prevails. But in the one case this object would be attained by charging all that the present traffic will bear, while in the other case it would be attained by lowering rates so as to undercut competitors.

[1] " Windom Committee," *Report, op. cit.*, pt. ii, p. 142; U. S. Industrial Commission, *Report*, vol. xix, p. 413; F. A. Delano, *Commercial and Financial Chronicle*, vol. civ (1917), p. 318; Carl Snyder, *American Railways as Investments* (New York, 1907), pp. 64-5; Frederick Strauss, *The Relation Between Capital and Rates—an Address delivered at the University Club, New York City, March 7, 1912* (Buffalo, etc., 1912).

Our conclusions, then, as to the effect of capitalization on rates, when these rates are fixed by the railways themselves, is that some relation may exist, but that this relation is much less direct and of much less significance than is generally assumed in popular discussions.

B. INFLUENCE OF CAPITALIZATION ON RATES UNDER GOVERNMENT CONTROL

In these days of strict government regulation. it is far more important to study the factors that influence our courts and commissions in their rate decisions than to discuss the rate-making policy of the railway management. For the government, not the railway, has the last word. General rate levels are now limited, not to what the traffic will bear, but rather to what the Interstate Commerce Commission or the United States Supreme Court will bear.

If regulating commissions were to allow railway companies to charge such rates as would earn interest and dividends on all outstanding securities, the relation between capitalization and rates would be obvious. But as a matter of fact, no such simple relation prevails; the connection is more indirect. In order to understand this connection, we must have in mind the general principles which guide a commission or a court in a rate case.

The starting point in the theory of rate regulation is the principle of common law, now supported by state and federal statutes, that public service enterprises must charge " reasonable " rates. Until very recently, no test of reasonableness has been set by statute. But in the United States a standard has been developed by the courts, under their authority to review all rate regulations to determine whether they violate the constitutional guaranties against confiscation of property. According to these court decisions, a company must ordinarily be allowed to charge sufficient rates to earn a " reasonable return " on the " fair

value of the property being used by it for the convenience of
the public." This so-called " valuation basis " of rate making has now been formally accepted by Congress, which has
provided in the present Transportation Act that the Interstate Commerce Commission shall fix such rates as will permit each group of carriers to earn a " fair return on the
aggregate value " of their railway property.[1]

In determining the influence of capitalization in a rate
case, we must pay regard to both of the above-mentioned
factors: "reasonable" (or "fair") return, and "fair
value." Does the amount of outstanding securities have
any effect on the rate of return that a commission or a
court would consider "reasonable?" Does it affect the
estimate of the "fair value" of the property? Each
of these questions must be answered before we can settle
the relation between capitalization and rates. Let us
consider these two points separately, first analyzing the
fair value, and later discussing the *rate of return* on that
value.

1. Capitalization and "Fair Value"

As every student of public utility problems knows, the
courts have never set any definite standard of " fair value "
for rate making. Usually they have accepted a valuation
based on a compromise of different possible tests. What
these tests may be is indicated in the leading case of Smyth
v. Ames.[2] The famous dictum in that case reads as follows:

[1] The Act provides that, for a period of two years beginning March
1, 1920, the Commission shall fix a " fair " return equivalent to a rate of
5½ per cent of the aggregate property value but may, in its discretion,
allow an additional half per cent to make provision for improvements.
At the end of the two-year period, the rate of return is to be fixed by
the Commission from time to time at such a point as the prevailing
conditions may justify.

[2] 169 U. S. 466, 545 (1898).

We hold, however, that the basis of all calculations as to the reasonableness of rates . . . . must be the fair value of the property being used by it for the convenience of the public. And in order to ascertain that value, the original cost of construction, the amount expended in permanent improvements, the amount and market value of its bonds and stock, the present as compared with the original cost of construction, the probable earning capacity of the property under particular rates prescribed by statute, and the sum required to meet operating expenses, are all matters for consideration, and are to be given such weight as may be just and right in each case.

On the basis of this dictum there are two distinct grounds on which the amount of capitalization might be given weight in estimating " fair value: " First, it might be taken as evidence of " the original cost of construction " and of the " amount expended in permanent improvements; " second, it might be held to constitute in itself a vested right, to be honored at its face value. This second interpretation might follow from the fact that the dictum refers to the " amount and market value of its bonds and stocks " as separate items to be considered, distinct from the item of original cost. Let us discuss first the use of capitalization as *evidence* of the actual cost of the property.

Capitalization as evidence of the actual investment. In the determination of " fair value " for rate-making purposes, courts have held that one of the most important elements to be considered is the original cost of the property. Indeed, the recent tendency, on the part of some commissions at least, has been to make it the controlling test—a tendency to which some authorities think that the courts will soon accede. Unfortunately, however, the railways of this country failed to keep accurate records of their capital costs until required to do so under the amendment of 1906 to the Interstate Commerce Act. So far from making correct entries of capital expenditures, many of the railways, prior to that date and to some extent even thereafter, deliberately made excessive charges to the capital account in order to conceal from the public and from the regulating commissions the true relation between profits and investment. The practice of stock watering went hand in hand with a practice of inflating the property accounts, which were written up so as to balance whatever amounts of securities the controlling interests might deem fit to issue.

In spite of its notorious inaccuracy, this nominal capitalization, to which the book values were made to correspond, has been the only record of actual costs possessed by the commissions and courts. Indeed, not only has capitalization been the only record of actual cost, but also, in the case of most railways, it has been the only test *of any sort* on which " fair value " might be based; for physical valuations have not yet been completed.

Faced with the necessity of deciding whether railroads should be allowed to raise their rates, and lacking any other information as to the fair value of the property, the Interstate Commerce Commission, in all its general rate cases, has been obliged to take account of capitalization as an evidence of the property value. To be sure, it has placed little confidence in the figures so obtained, and has therefore attempted to discount them as far as possible. But in the absence of other data, it has been compelled to base its decisions largely on these faulty statements.[1] Recognition of the unsatisfac-

[1] The above statement was written before the recent rate decision, dated July 29, 1920, granting to all carriers a heavy increase in freight and passenger rates. This new decision goes farther than any previous case in accepting capitalization or book value as the controlling factor in the determination of fair value. As compared to a book value of $20,040,572,611, the " fair value " was found by the commission to be $18,900,000,000. A review of earlier decisions by the Interstate Commission with reference to capitalization as an element in " fair value " will be found in Appendix A, *infra.*

tory character of such evidence is what led the commission to urge upon Congress the necessity of a physical valuation. When this valuation has been completed, the commission may be expected to disregard entirely the outstanding securities in its estimate of the property value.

Whether the physical valuation, when completed, will show that the railways have been making excessive profits in the past is of course a matter for conjecture. Railway men, however, confidently assert that total net capitalization of American railways will be found to be under rather than over the total "physical value" as based on replacement cost. It must be admitted that preliminary reports on the valuation of several of the railways tend to bear out this contention.[1] But this of course raises the whole question whether public utilities should be valued for rate-making purposes on the basis of their present high replacement cost, or on the basis of their much lower original cost. In the latter case, the outstanding capitalization is almost certainly excessive. The present treatise will not discuss this perplexing question of rate making.

Although no one can deny that in the past, overcapitalization has been used deliberately as a means of deceiving the government and the public as to the actual cost of the property, one need not conclude that it may always be so used. It is entirely conceivable that the railways might be permitted to water their stock without limit, while being compelled to state correctly on their balance sheets the actual property investments. In that case, an excessive stock issue would be offset on the balance sheet by a corresponding entry to "Stock Discount." Under such a procedure, the property account would state correctly the actual

[1] For detailed statistics on this point, see the testimony of Thomas W. Hulme before the Interstate Commerce Commission, Washington, May 26th and 27th, 1920, separately printed by the Secretary, Presidents' Conference Committee, Philadelphia, June 4, 1920.

cost, with the result that courts and commissions would not be deceived if they desired to base rates on the actual investment. Precisely that practice has prevailed in England. British railways have been permitted to issue large amounts of watered stock, but in their reports to the Board of Trade they have been obliged to state frankly the amount of water. Not so, however, with American railways. They have balanced their excessive stock issues, not by charges to Stock Discount, but rather by an overvaluation of their property. It is this deliberate deception that has made stock watering as practised in America so much more vicious than stock watering in England.[1]

Capitalization as a separate factor in " fair value." For anyone who is not versed in the legal profundities of railway counsel, it may be difficult to see how nominal capitalization can be claimed as an element in fair value except in so far as it may indicate the actual investment. Yet railway spokesmen have repeatedly argued that the amount of outstanding securities should be given weight in determining fair value, entirely irrespective of the actual cost. The basis of this plea is the " innocent investor " argument. Even if securities are fictitious, they have been bought in good faith by investors who supposed that they represented real property. These investors, it is held, should not be " penalized " for the sins of bygone financiers.

During the recent general rate cases,—the " Five Per Cent," and the " Fifteen Per Cent " cases,—the financial and railway interests set going a wave of propaganda urging this claim for the protection of existing securities. The nature of their argument is indicated in an address before the Investment Bankers Association of America by its president, Mr. A. B. Leach. Mr. Leach's remarks are reported as follows:

[1] But even the British practice has not escaped criticism ; see pp. 60-61, *infra.*

A very strong and able committee of our members attended
a session of the Interstate Commerce Commission when the
earlier railroad rate question was under consideration.   They
presented, with all due emphasis, that the investors' position in
relation to the rate question is that the railroads should be
granted the increase asked for, whatever may have been the
error or failures or mistakes of mind or purpose in issuing some
of these securities, the fact remains that the railroads have become very important, if not the most important industry in the
country, and the investments in railroad securities form a very
large percentage of the security for the savings of our people,
in more than one way.[1]

One would not be justified, however, in assuming that
commissions actually take account of outstanding securities
simply because investors plead for such consideration.
Railway interests, in rate cases, have continually entered
pleas which commissions have continually denied.   We must
turn, therefore, to the decisions of courts and commissions
to see whether these pleas have won recognition.

On this point the theory of the law is sufficiently clear.
The United States Supreme Court has held that public
utilities are entitled to a return on the " fair value " of the
property, not on the securities issued against that property.[2]
To be sure, the above-quoted dictum in Smyth *v.* Ames
states that in the determination of the fair value of a company's property, " the amount and market value of its bonds
and stocks " are among the elements to be considered.   But

[1] *Proceedings of the Association of Investment Bankers of America,
Denver, September, 1915,* pp. 15-16.

[2] This statement applies to securities that have not been issued under
the specific authorization of a public service commission. Whether or
not securities, when officially approved by a commission, will create
a legal claim in rate decisions has not as yet been settled in court.
The public utility laws contain a disclaimer of any obligation or guaranty
on the part of the state with respect to authorized securities; but some
authorities are doubtful as to the complete efficacy of this disclaimer.

later decisions have been unanimous in holding that this statement did not imply the right to earn profits on fictitious securities. Indeed, quite the contrary view was expressed in the Smyth case itself, as well as in subsequent decisions. So generally recognized is this point of view today, that we need spend no time here in following the court decisions. However, further citations are given in Appendix A of this study.

Public service commissions, no less than courts, have been almost unanimous in asserting that capitalization is not of itself an element in " fair value." Some years ago, to be sure, the Interstate Commerce Commission, in the Spokane Rate Case,[1] appeared to be taking a contrary position, acknowledging the claim of outstanding securities, even when watered. But this position seems later to have been entirely reversed.[2]

Few authorities today would question the statement that *in the theory of the law,* at least, a capitalization in excess of actual assets should have no consideration in fixing the " fair value " of the property. But it is often maintained by persons familiar with the procedure of rate cases that, despite all theory, courts and commissions do give weight to the claim for a return on excessive security issues. The " innocent investor " plea is thought to have some influence.

It is extremely difficult, if not impossible, definitely to prove or to disprove this opinion by reference to the published reports of rate cases. For in fixing a valuation, commissions do not state what, if any, allowance has been made for watered securities. If such allowance is made, it does not so appear in the report, but is probably covered up by an excessive estimate of the value of intangibles, such as " over-

---

[1] 15 I. C. C. Rep. 376, 410 (1909).

[2] See Appendix A for a discussion of the position of the Interstate Commerce Commission and of various state commissions.

head charges," or "going value." Only those who have taken part in the proceedings can really know whether or not capitalization has influenced the decision.

It is therefore very significant to find testimony from behind the scenes to the effect that outstanding securities are in fact taken into account. Members of the Interstate Commerce Commission and of various state commissions have expressed this view. In an address before the National Association of Railway Commissioners, Interstate Commerce Commissioner Clements remarked:

It is often said that capitalization has nothing to do with the question of reasonable rates. Perhaps legally and technically speaking that is true, but as a matter of fact it is never left out of view.[1]

On another occasion, Mr. Clark, Chairman of the Interstate Commerce Commission, expressed a similar view.[2]

At the conference of the National Association of Railway Commissioners for 1913. there was presented a symposium of opinions from various commissioners on questions of security regulation.[3] Of the six commissioners who expressed an opinion on the influence of capitalization in valuation cases, five believed that such influence existed, and only one, Mr. Roemer of the Wisconsin Commission, seemed to take the opposite view.

Such testimony from men who have themselves taken part in regulating rates can hardly be gainsaid. One is forced to conclude that excessive capitalization, all legal theory to the contrary, has caused courts and commissions

---

[1] *Proceedings*, 24th Convention, 1912, p. 219.

[2] U. S. Congress, House of Rep., Committee on Interstate and Foreign Commerce, *Hearings*, February 9 to March 17, 1914, *op. cit.*, pp. 57-87.

[3] *Proceedings*, 25th Convention, 1913, pp. 115-223, 238-257.

to be more liberal in their valuations than they would otherwise have been.

But without denying this past influence of capitalization
on " fair value," one may seriously question whether any
such connection need prevail in the future.   The very idea
of counting nominal liabilities as part of the amount of
property on which a return should be earned is so illogical
and so absurd that it would hardly have had any currency
except under peculiar circumstances.   These circumstances
have been the chaotic condition of the theory and practice
of rate regulation.   In the first place, no clear-cut basis of
valuation has ever been adopted by commissions or accepted
by the courts.   In the second place, no adequate records of
original or replacement cost have been at hand.   The
natural result of this unsettled state of things has been to
put the courts and commissions in a compromising frame
of mind.   Almost any plea that counsel for the companies
might present would, in some vague way, be taken into account; to use the judicial phraseology, it would " be given
such weight as may be just and right in each case."   But
this chaotic condition will not last.   As soon as the government adopts a definite standard of valuation, and as soon as
it secures the necessary records of cost, it will have removed
the uncertainties that have caused rate regulators to
take account of security issues in estimating " fair value."

Conclusions on capitalization and " fair value."   The
following conclusions may now be set forth as to the
relation between capitalization and " fair value " for rate
making.   The amount of outstanding securities has been
a factor in valuation proceedings, first, as evidence of the
actual investment, and second, as an item entitled to some
weight on its own account.   The latter consideration, however, is not explicitly stated in the decisions of courts and
commissions, and one is left to infer its influence from the

unofficial remarks of commissioners. But, although capitalization has been, on both of the above grounds, an element in valuation, there is no good reason to suppose that it need continue to remain an important factor in the future. For after a physical valuation has been completed, and after a definite basis of rate-making value has been set, courts and commissions will have no reason or excuse for accepting the par value of securities as an indication of the " fair value."

If one were to assume that the evil of stock watering lay simply and solely in a resulting overvaluation of railway property for rate-making purposes, one might fairly question whether the most expedient way to cure the evil would not be to prevent the overvaluation without troubling to prevent the stock watering.[1] Government regulation of security issues is a costly experiment, and in some respects a dangerous experiment. Would it not be wiser, then, to leave the private railway managements free to determine the amount of securities, and simply to require that any excessive issues must not be permitted to inflate the property accounts? In short, could not stock watering be made innocuous by full publicity of the actual investment?

Several eminent authorities have answered this question in the affirmative. The Railroad Securities Commission took such a position when it reported in favor of publicity rather than of regulation of railway finance. Similar views

---

[1] Some years ago, a bill to secure this object was introduced into Congress by Representative Adamson. Mr. Adamson was at that time opposed to the plan for federal regulation of railway securities. As a substitute for such a measure, he introduced a bill providing that if any railroad should plead inadequacy of return on its securities as a reason for being permitted to raise its rates, it must present evidence that those securities represent actual investment (*Cong. Debates*, 61st Cong., 2nd Sess., 1910, vol. cv, pp. 5592-4). A somewhat similar proposal was made by Mr. S. Z. Mitchell, President of the Electric Bond and Share Company, at a hearing of the Senate Committee on Interstate Commerce, December 14, 1915.

have been expressed by Mr. Balthasar H. Meyer[1] of the Interstate Commerce Commission, and by Mr. Franklin K. Lane.[2]

The position taken by these authorities would be strong indeed were it not for the fact that the evil of overcapitalization is not confined to its possible influence on the valuation of the property. Even though that influence were completely removed, other evils would remain. What these evils are we shall note in the remaining sections of this chapter.

2. *Capitalization and the Rate of Return*

When a commission has found the "fair value" of a railroad property, it must next determine the rate of return which the company is entitled to earn on that value. The courts have held that this return must be " reasonable; " but their decisions as to what constitutes reasonableness have been even more indefinite than have been their decisions on " fair value."[3] The tendency of the courts, however, has been to leave the commissions much more discretion in the former matter than in the latter.[4] Beyond insisting on a certain minimum,—say 5 or 6 per cent,—the courts have not been disposed to hold that any rate fixed by a commission is confiscatory. Our study of the effect of capitalization on the rate of return must therefore emphasize the practice of commissions rather than the rulings of courts.

---

[1] U. S. House of Representatives, Committee on Interstate and Foreign Commerce, *Hearings, February 9 to March 17, 1914, on " Regulation of the Issuance of Stocks and Bonds,"* pp. 87-114.

[2] " Railroad Capitalization and Federal Regulation," *American Review of Reviews*, vol. xxxvii (1908), pp. 711-14.

[3] On the rate of return, see Robert H. Whitten, *Valuation of Public Service Corporations*, 2 vols. (New York, 1912-14), vol. i, ch. xxx, vol. ii, ch. xxx; Beale and Wyman, *Railroad Rate Regulation*, 2nd ed., by Bruce Wyman (New York, 1915), ch. vii.

[4] Whitten, vol. i, p. 690.

In fixing the rate of return, public service commissions must take account of two different considerations: The one is the question of fairness to the investors; the other is that of public expediency. Is the given return a fair compensation for the use of the present investment? If so, is it sufficient to attract new capital into the business? Both of these questions must be answered before deciding what rates a public utility should be allowed to charge.[1] To be sure, the distinction between what is "fair" and what is "expedient" is not always made; often, perhaps usually, these two factors would be considered identical. But at times there is a distinction of much importance. Let us discuss first the question of the *fair* rate and later the question of the *expedient rate*.

The Fair Rate. While decisions as to what constitutes a fair rate do not all agree, the generally accepted principle is this: that the rate should be such as would induce the investment of capital in similar enterprises, similarly situated. If, for example, five per cent will attract capital into eastern railways, then five per cent would be a "fair return" for that class of enterprise. If, on the other hand, eight or ten per cent would be required for western roads, then that higher rate would be "fair" for such an investment.

How, then, may this rate of return be affected by nominal capitalization? Only in a very indirect way; namely, through the possible effect of capitalization on the credit of the railways. The fact that many railways have been overcapitalized, and otherwise financially mismanaged, may bring railway investments into disrepute, and may therefore raise the rate of return that is necessary to attract

[1] That is to say, the *commissions* must pay regard to both of these questions; on the other hand, the *courts* usually take account merely of the first point.

capital into that class of enterprise. An artificial element of
risk is created—the risk that railway companies may be
found to be financially topheavy; and investors may fairly
demand that the public should pay them a higher rate of
return for assuming that risk.

That this relation between capitalization and the rate
of return may not be merely theoretical will be recognized
by impartial students of American railway finance. Fiascos
like Rock Island, Alton, and Frisco, caused largely by reckless overcapitalization, have helped to bring all railway investments into disrepute, and have therefore tended to raise
the rate of interest that must be offered to attract capital.
The fact that, up to the present time, railways have perhaps
not secured this necessary rate, and that therefore capital
has not been attracted, is a temporary situation which does
not disprove the ultimate relation between capitalization and
the rate of return.

But of much more significance than the relation of capitalization to the *fair* rate is its relation to the *expedient* rate
—the rate that may exceed what is considered " fair." To
this question we now turn.

The expedient rate. In the previous paragraphs we
noted that commissions have generally held that a " fair
rate " of return on public service property is that rate which
will attract capital into enterprises of a similar nature.
Ordinarily, this would also be the " expedient " rate; that
is, it would be the minimum rate needed in order to maintain the good credit of the company and its power to give
adequate service. But sometimes the " fair rate " would
not be sufficient for this purpose. Let us suppose that the
company in question is seriously overcapitalized; that its
earnings under present rates are barely sufficient to enable
it to pay its interest charges and thus to escape bankruptcy.
A company in this condition will be able to borrow

money, if at all, only by paying exorbitant rates of interest. It would be quite unable to secure this money if it were allowed to earn merely the " fair rate," *i. e.,* the rate current in other railways similarly located but more conservatively capitalized.

As an illustration of this fact, let us take the New Haven.[1] In the year 1915, this road, despite its run-down physical condition, reported earnings equal to 6.2 per cent of the book value of its railway property.[2] Yet, while such a return might well have been considered a " fair rate," it was quite too small to support the company's credit in view of its heavy liabilities; nor did it suffice to prevent President Elliott from complaining bitterly that the public service commissions were not sufficiently liberal in their rate decisions.

Commissions have frequently been obliged to face such situations in fixing rates that apply to weak railways and public utilities. They are confronted with this dilemma: that they must either sanction exorbitant rates or else accept the consequence of poor service. Which horn of the dilemma have they chosen? That is a difficult question to answer. The difficulty lies in the fact that commissions, in their rate decisions, have seldom made a clear-cut distinction between what is fair and what is expedient. They have never decided, for example, that a particular company should be allowed only five per cent as a " fair " rate of return, but that seven per cent should be allowed in order to maintain the corporate credit. On the contrary, they have fixed a so-called " reasonable " rate, without stating the extent to which necessity rather than fairness has been the

---

[1] To be sure, the New Haven was not overcapitalized in the narrow sense of that term. But it was nevertheless financially overweighted because of the burden of its unprofitable outside enterprises.

[2] 4 Ann. Rep. Mass. P. S. C. 324 (1916). See also 21 I. C. C. Rep. 62 (1914).

test of the reasonableness. This is perfectly natural in view of the uncertain and indefinite standards that have prevailed as to what is fair. It is doubtful whether the commissions know themselves just to what extent justice and to what extent public policy is their guide in fixing the rate.

But for all this uncertainty, a study of recent rate cases leaves no doubt that excessive returns have sometimes been permitted in order to bolster up the credit of overcapitalized or mismanaged companies. In this respect, commissions seem to have differed in their attitudes. The Interstate Commerce Commission and the Massachusetts Public Service Commission have taken the position, in theory at least, that they are not empowered by law to permit excessive rates for the sake of upholding railway credit. On the other hand, several state commissions have interpreted their powers more liberally. They have held that the paramount consideration is adequate service, and that as between poor service and excessive rates, the latter is the lesser of the two evils.

In Appendix B of this study the reader will find a review of the position of various public service commisssions on this point. On the whole, one notes a recent tendency to pay more and more attention to the question of expediency and less to the abstract question of fairness. The tendency has been especially prominent during the war and has continued since the armistice as a result of the alarming decline in the credit of railroads and street railways.[1]

---

[1] The distinction between what is fair and what is expedient is clearly brought out in the present efforts of street railway companies to secure permission to charge a higher fare than is stipulated in their franchises. Since the old charge had been fixed by voluntary agreement between the two parties to the franchise, it must be regarded, according to current business principles, as the " fair " charge. To be sure, it has not proved sufficient, in these times of high operating costs, to earn a " fair return on the fair value of the property." But

RAILROAD CAPITALIZATION

C. CONCLUSIONS ON THE EFFECT OF CAPITALIZATION
ON RATES

The various ways in which capitalization may affect railway rates have been discussed. These may now be summarized in outline form.

Overcapitalization may affect rates:

I. When rates are fixed by the railway management,

  (1) Under monopoly conditions, by causing the management to adopt the short-sighted policy of charging high rates in order to secure maximum returns in the immediate future, instead of charging lower rates in the expectation of building up traffic in the long run.

  (2) Under competitive conditions, by causing the management to adopt the equally short-sighted policy of cutting rates unduly so as to secure a temporary advantage over competitors.

II. When rates are fixed by government authority,

  (1) By raising the valuation on which the rates are based,
    a. through the use of capitalization as evidence of the original investment,

in these cases, "fair return" is not the test of the "fair" charge. Doubtless, each party to the contract considered the prospective return before agreeing to the five-cent fare. But once the contract is signed, the company is entitled to whatever earnings it can make out of the given charge, no more, no less. If profits had been excessive, as they might have been in a period of falling operating expenses, the cities would have had no right to demand a reduction in the fare. Similarly, the fact that profits have proved to be inadequate gives the companies no claim for relief from their burdensome contract. As a matter of strict justice they should take their losses, just as a stock trader takes his loss when he has made an unfavorable contract to buy or to sell. But the question cannot be settled on the basis of strict justice; for the public, no less than the railway companies, may suffer from an enforcement of the contract. Expediency may dictate leniency toward the railway companies just as it may sometimes require leniency on the part of a creditor toward his bankrupt debtor.

       b. through the tendency of courts and commissions
       to accept the amount of securities as constituting,
       per se, an element in the " fair value,"
(2) By raising the rate of return which companies must
       be permitted to earn, because of the tendency of
       overcapitalization to weaken the corporate credit,
       and thus by affecting
       a. the " fair rate," *i. e.,* the rate necessary to attract
       capital into similar enterprises,
       b. the " expedient rate," *i. e.,* the rate necessary to
       attract capital into the particular enterprise in
       question.

Since rates are now subject to strict regulation by the
government, the relations listed in the second division of the
above outline are the only ones of present importance.
Under government control of rates, capitalization may affect transportation charges in two ways: first, by influencing
the " fair value" of the property as fixed by a court or a
commission; second, by influencing the rate of return that
a company may be permitted to earn. But the relation of
capitalization to " fair value," while it has doubtless been
present in the past, need not continue in the future provided
that the railways are required to keep accurate records of
actual investment. As an argument for security regulation,
therefore, the presence of such a connection in the past cannot be considered of much weight. With respect to the
rate of return, however, the influence of capitalization cannot be so easily overcome. The fact cannot be denied that a
financially weak railway—whether that weakness is due to
overcapitalization or to any other cause—cannot secure the
funds for developing its business without paying an exorbitant rate of interest. The public, then, must either pay that
interest in higher rates or must suffer the poor service that
will result from a failure to secure the capital.

It is true that there may sometimes be a third alternative. Instead of permitting a financially weak railway to charge excessive rates, a commission might keep down the rates to the minimum and thus force the railway into a receivership and a reorganization. That heroic method may be the very best solution, but it cannot be considered an adequate one, for two reasons: first, because bankruptcy brings discredit, not merely on the particular company, but also on all railway enterprises; second, because a weak company may not be quite weak enough to be forced into receivership. For years the company may lead a hand-to-mouth existence on the low rates, and a commission may be powerless either to make it give good service or to compel a reorganization.

II. Effect of Capitalization on Service

Overcapitalization, we have just seen, must lead to one of two things, if not to both: excessive rates, or inferior service. Most of the popular discussions have emphasized the first result. Yet, of the two, the latter is much the more serious. A financially weak railway is far more likely to reduce its standards of service and to neglect necessary improvements than it is to raise its rates. The former policy is the easy one; the latter presents many difficulties. But in spite of its greater practical importance, the relation of capitalization to service may be discussed much more briefly than the relation of capitalization to rates, since it is simpler and subject to less controversy.

There are two chief reasons why poor service rather than high rates has been the more frequent outcome of overcapitalization. In the first place, competition has prevented a financially weak road from charging higher rates than its competitors. This accounts for the fact, already noted, that highly capitalized railways like the Rock Island, the Alton, and the Chicago Great Western, have charged relatively low rates. In the second place, commissions have been reluctant to allow weak companies to bolster their credit by charging excessive rates. Perhaps, as we have already suggested, this reluctance may become somewhat less strong in the future; yet it will doubtless always be present to some degree.

The history of practically all recent railroad failures illustrates the effect of financial weakness on the quality of the service. Unable to secure funds, these roads struggled along for years without making necessary additions and improvements, meanwhile permitting their existing facilities to deteriorate by deferring maintenance charges. When finally the companies did fail and go into receiverships, the receivers had [or were obliged] to devote all available resources to getting the road and equipment back into fair operating condition.

Recent reorganizations have required large sums for rehabilitation despite the difficulty of securing the necessary subscriptions or payments on assessment. According to Daggett, the Frisco secured for this purpose nearly eleven million dollars; the Chicago and Great Western set aside $9,892,274 to cover cost of rehabilitation, additional terminals. equipment, and shops; the Missouri Pacific provided $12,713,792 for additional working capital, new equipment and immediate improvements, as well as for adjustment expenses and the payment of loans.[1]

Everyone is familiar with the unsatisfactory service of the New England roads since their financial difficulties.[2] Commenting on this condition, the Massachusetts Public Service Commission said:

[1] "Recent Railroad Failures and Reorganizations," *Quarterly Journal of Economics*, vol. xxxii (1918), pp. 446-86, 465.

[2] For a discussion of the inferior service on the New Haven and the Boston and Maine, see 27 I. C. C. Rep. 560 (1913); 3 Ann. Rep. Mass. P. S. C. xii (1915); 4 Mass. P. S. C. Rep. 319-330 (1916).

Along with the increase in rates, passenger service has been substantially curtailed, more particularly upon the New York, New Haven and Hartford and Boston and Maine Railroads, a curtailment made necessary by the financial difficulties of the companies. In view of the fact that these difficulties were in no small measure due, not to causes beyond control, but to past mismanagement, the forbearance and patience of the traveling and shipping public in the face of higher rates and lessened service has been noteworthy.[1]

The ill effects of gross overcapitalization are familiar to all patrons of the New York street railway system.[2]   When the Public Service Commission was considering the reorganization plans of the Third Avenue Railway, in 1910, that company was still using horse cars on some of its lines. " For five years preceding the receivership." says Professor Ripley, " not a new car was bought; and it was beyond the power of the company to buy."[3]   That financial abuses were responsible for this run-down condition was admitted by Receiver Whitridge, in spite of his insistence that the public should not concern itself with the regulation of future security issues.   The Public Service Commission quotes him as saying that "the endeavor to pay interest on what was fairly called watered stock, or stock out of which the value had run, resulted in deterioration of service, inadequacy of service. . . ."[4]   He qualified this remark, however, by expressing the belief that this inferior service need not have occurred, even with overcapitalization, if the Public Service Commission had been in existence; but unfortunately this opinion has not been borne out by later experience.

---

[1] 3 Ann. Rep. Mass. P. S. C. xiii (1915).

[2] Ripley, *Railroads, Finance and Organization,* describes this situation and cites further references (pp. 283, 286-7). See also the decisions of the New York Public Service Commission, 1st District, on the " First and Second Reorganization Plans of the Third Avenue Railroad" (2 P. S. C. R. [1st Dist. N. Y.] 94, 347).

[3] Ripley, p. 283.

[4] 2 P. S. C. R. (1st Dist. N. Y.) 94, 117 (1909).

In 1914 the *Railway Age Gazette,* referring to four railroads in financial difficulties—the Wabash, the Frisco, the Rock Island, and the Missouri Pacific—remarked:

No one of the four properties is in bad shape physically; on the other hand, no one of the four properties has been kept abreast of the modern sciences of railroading, not through any mistaken ideas on the part of the operating management, but simply because of lack of money and of what have been considered the exigencies of the case.[1]

This statement may also be applied to the entire former Gould system. It would be especially pertinent with respect to the Missouri, Kansas and Texas Railway. On the condition of this road Mr. J. W. Kendrick, who investigated the property for Speyer & Co., bankers, reported as follows:

[The railway was] handicapped by extraordinary interest charges upon an accumulated nondescript indebtedness, so large as to make it necessary to starve the property with respect to maintenance in order to keep it solvent, especially in view of the fact that the payment of dividends was commenced in 1906 and continued until 1914, during which time $4,160,000 was dispensed to stockholders that should have been returned to the property in the form of well-conceived improvements. . . .[2]

Of course, it would not be correct to assume that in all these cases the financial weakness that was responsible for the inadequate service was caused wholly by overcapitalization or by other forms of financial abuse. The causes of railroad failure have been diverse; excessive competition has been an important factor,[3] and in not a few cases, unjust

[1] *Railway Age Gazette,* vol. lvi (1914), p. 1174.

[2] *Ibid.,* vol. lxii (1917), p. 365.

[3] Referring to failures since 1907, Daggett says: "Generally speaking, the failures were in the intensely competitive territory of the Central Freight Association, and in the less densely settled sections west and southwest of the Mississippi River" (*Quarterly Journal of Economics,* vol. xxxii [1918], p. 448.)

rate regulation must share the blame.   But it is none the
less true that in all of the instances mentioned above, and in
most of the other recent cases of receivership, overcapitalization has been an important factor in the trouble.[1]

Up to the present point, we have been referring simply to
the inadequate service on those railways that have been conspicuous examples either of dishonest or of unwise financial
practice.   These cases in themselves make up a large aggregate.   Of 34,559 miles of line in receivers' hands in December 1916, over forty per cent were reported by the Interstate Commerce Commission to have " suffered principally
from financial mismanagement and exploitation." [2]   A still
greater proportion have been subject to imprudent, even
when not dishonest, financing.   But even more serious, perhaps, is the weakened credit of American railways as
a whole.   The general lack of adequate facilities, particularly
of equipment and terminals, is notorious.   Indeed, no persons
have recognized this shortcoming nor deplored the loss of
credit which it has occasioned. more than the railway representatives themselves.   Only the cause of this financial mis-
fortune is the subject of dispute.   Railway men have minimized the factor of improper financial methods and have
ascribed most of their difficulties to unfair regulation.   In
support of this argument they point out that only a small
minority of the railways of the country have been guilty of
dishonest practices.   Public service commissions, on the
other hand, deny their responsibility for the trouble and place
the blame on overcapitalization. undue expansion, and
financial abuses.   In reply to the argument that only a

[1] For a discussion of the causes of recent railroad failures, see
Daggett, *op. cit.*, also, Fankhauser, " Receivership and Reorganization
of Steam Railroads," printed as an appendix to the " Newlands Committee" *Hearings* (vol. ii, pp. 1937-2138).   For failures prior to 1907,
see Daggett, *Railroad Reorganizations* (Boston, 1908).

[2] 44 I. C. C. Rep. 223.

small number of the railways have committed financial sins, they assert that these cases bring disrepute and suspicion upon all companies, good and bad, and so injure the credit of American railway investments as a whole.[1]

It is quite unnecessary for our present purpose to decide upon the exact weight of these opposing views. Sufficiently clear in any case is the fact that improper capitalization has been *one* of the serious causes, even though by no means the only cause, of the recent financial difficulties. In fact, the need for a more liberal governmental policy toward the railways can hardly be treated apart from the need for a wiser policy of railway finance. The public cannot be expected to sanction liberal rate increases unless it receives better assurance than it has received in the past that the increased earnings will be used more honestly and more prudently in the effort to maintain the credit of the companies. This point seems now to be recognized by the spokesmen for the railways, to judge from their recent acceptance of federal control of security issues as a necessary part of railway regulation.

III. Conclusions of Chapter[2]

The discussion in this chapter, it is hoped, will serve to show how unwarranted is the assertion, until recently made by most railway officials, that the capitalization of railway companies is not a public concern. And yet, it is equally clear that the influence of the amount of outstanding

[1] These two sides of the case were argued at length at the hearings of the "Newlands Committee" by Mr. Thom, Counsel for the Railway Executives' Advisory Committee, and by Mr. Thelen, President of the National Association of Railway Commissioners. See also U. S. House of Rep., Committee on Interstate and Foreign Commerce, *Hearings on "Federal Operation of Transportation Systems,"* 65th Cong., 2d Sess., January 8-29, 1918.

[2] A more detailed summary of the conclusions as to the influence of capitalization on rates has been given already, pp. 36-38, *supra*.

securities is by no means as direct as is frequently assumed by railway critics. The medium of this influence is credit. Credit forms the connecting link between capitalization on the one hand, and rates and service on the other. It is the failure to appreciate the indirect nature of this connection that has been responsible for the conflicting views on the subject. That improper capitalization is injurious to corporate credit would be denied by no one; on the other hand, that poor credit is prejudicial to the interests of the public is recognized by all. The conclusion that capitalization must therefore be a matter of public concern would seem to follow as a matter of course. Yet for years it has been vigorously denied by railway spokesmen. In almost the same breath they have asserted the need for higher rates in order to support railway credit, while denying the need for sound capitalization to further the same object.

But while the foregoing conclusions justify the public suspicion of stock watering, they also indicate that a shift of emphasis is required in explaining the evil and in providing a cure. The assumption has been that there is a direct and close relation between capitalization and rates—the higher the former, the higher the latter. Now this assumption would be true if the amount of securities were accepted as a test of " fair value." But this test has been only partly accepted in the past, and in the future the government need not accept it at all, if it does not wish to do so. In the future, then, the only serious danger from overcapitalization will be, not that it will be an element in determining fair value, but rather that it will injure credit. But that raises a new question. What is the exact relation between capitalization and corporate credit? Is it simply that low capitalization tends to create sound credit, and high capitalization to create weak credit? Or is the relation more complex? To this question is devoted the following chapter, on the Influence of Capitalization on Railway Credit.

CHAPTER II

The Influence of Capitalization on Railway Credit

In the preceding chapter, the conclusion was reached that overcapitalization results in higher rates or in inferior service to the extent that it injures the corporate credit. It remains to consider in the present chapter the ways in which such injury may occur.

According to a prevalent view, there is an inverse relation between a company's capitalization and its financial soundness—low capitalization tends to cause good credit, high capitalization to cause poor credit. As a very rough generalization, this statement may be allowed to pass; but it is subject to qualifications of such importance that it cannot be accepted as a satisfactory guide to financial practice.

Overcapitalization tends to weaken corporate credit, not directly because of the heavy nominal liabilities, but simply because those liabilities are apt to create excessive interest and dividend charges. But the relation between the capitalization and the amount of capital charges is not close. A company with an absurdly high capitalization may have a lighter burden of interest and dividends than a company capitalized at a low figure. In the former case, the rate of interest and dividends may be lower than in the latter case, so as more than to offset the difference in the amount of securities. Moreover, the highly capitalized company may have issued large amounts of stock but only a small amount of bonds and may therefore be able to make its payments contingent upon the earnings, while the undercapitalized company may have incurred a heavy debt and may be unable on that account to reduce its fixed charges in times of financial stress.

For these reasons it is necessary to take even more account of the *kind* of capitalization than of its total *amount*. Let us therefore discuss separately the three chief classes of securities: bonds (and other evidences of indebtedness), preferred stock, and common stock. With respect to each, we must consider how the amount of the issue may affect the capital charges and, hence, the credit of the issuing company. The first two classes, however, will be treated very briefly, since the evils of an overissue of bonds or of preferred stock are well recognized; but the last class—common stock—will require careful study, as it involves questions subject to much dispute.

(1) Bonds and Other Evidences of Indebtedness

A fundamental distinction has already been noted between bonds and stocks, or rather between debt capital and share capital. It is a distinction recognized in theory by everyone, yet, as the Railroad Securities Commission pointed out, too frequently ignored in its application to security regulation.[1] Bonds represent a promise to pay certain definite amounts of principal and interest. Default on these payments makes a company liable to receivership and foreclosure. Shares of stock, on the other hand, carry no such rigid obligations; their dividends are contingent upon earnings.

Because of this distinction, an excessive debt is generally a menace to credit of much more serious character than is an overissue of stock. Many financiers, indeed, would deny that the amount of common stock is of any material concern, but no one could dispute the evil of overindebtedness.

[1] *Report*, pp. 9-10.

How much more importance is attached by financiers to the amount of corporate debt than to the total capitalization may be seen by a study of railroad reorganizations. In perhaps the majority of cases where railways have been reorganized as a result of a failure, the fixed charges have been scaled down, but the total capitalization has been increased.[1] The reason for this is evident. A reduction in fixed charges was imperative; but the railway creditors could be induced to accept this reduction only by the offer of large amounts of preferred and common stocks. In addition, still more stock had to be issued—and issued freely—in order to induce the old stockholders to pay their assessments and to furnish the funds needed to rehabilitate the property. Doubtless the reorganization managers have often regretted the necessity of adding to an already excessive capitalization by such liberal distributions of stock, but they have been obliged to choose the lesser of two evils.

To some extent, state governments as well as financiers have recognized the peculiar dangers of an overissue of bonds; but they have been much less disposed to accept that fact as an excuse for excessive issues of stock. Indeed, the state policy has been criticized on this very point by able authorities, who have argued that the rigid restrictions which some states have imposed on the issuance of stock has forced railway companies to secure funds almost entirely by borrowing.[2] In later chapters we shall have occasion

[1] Formerly this was the case with the large majority of railway reorganizations; but the recent tendency has been toward a more conservative recapitalization. Daggett lists fifteen reorganizations that fall within the decade 1907-1917, of which eight resulted in a decrease in total capitalization and seven in an increase ("Recent Railroad Failures and Reorganizations," *Quarterly Journal of Economics*, vol. xxxii [1918], p. 469). The earlier reorganizations are treated by the same authority in his *Railroad Reorganization* (Boston, 1908).

[2] This view was expressed in the *Report of the Railroad Securities Commission*, pp. 10, 24.

to note the force of this criticism and to consider ways of meeting the difficulty.[1]

(2) Preferred Stock

The broad distinction noted above between bonds and stocks must be qualified in order to make room for a security that, in some respects, comes between the two main classes. Preferred stocks, like all other stocks, have a claim to returns only when earned—their dividends may be passed without giving shareholders the right to demand a receivership. But they differ from common stock, and resemble bonds, in that a definite rate of dividends is fixed. The same may be said of income bonds, which are not very different from certain kinds of preferred stocks. Because the rate of dividends is fixed, an excessive issue of preferred stock is a more serious burden than an overissue of common stock : the excess cannot so easily be offset by a corresponding reduction of the dividend rate. Of course it is always possible to pass the preferred dividends or to reduce them below the stipulated rate. But this procedure reacts so unfavorably upon a company's credit that directors do not follow it except under considerable financial stress.

Even more serious, perhaps, than the direct loss of credit resulting from the passing of preferred dividends is the temptation *not to pass them* when they should be passed. Funds that ought to be devoted to maintenance or improvement of the property are diverted to pay capital charges. This point is illustrated by the policy of the Frisco just prior to its failure in 1913. That company continued to pay dividends on its five million dollars of preferred stock up to within two months of the application for a receivership.[2]

[1] *Infra*, p. 94 *et seq.*

[2] Dividends were declared for the quarter ending March 31; the receivership was applied for on May 27.

When the preferential rights of the shares are cumulative, an excessive issue is all the more dangerous. If unpaid dividends are allowed to accumulate for several years, the common stock loses practically all value except for purposes of control, and even the preferred shares take on a highly speculative character. Neither cumulative preferred stocks nor cumulative income bonds have been widely used in American railway finance, although the former have been extensively employed by local public utility companies. In several recent railway reorganizations, however, they have been issued in order to avoid heavy fixed charges.[1] One may seriously doubt whether in the long run this conversion of fixed interest into cumulative dividend claims will be a gain. Daggett, an eminent authority on receiverships, thinks that the advantage is very questionable. "Railroads," he says, "are to some extent protected by it against formal bankruptcy, yet such formal bankruptcy is often better than the piling up of a huge load of unpaid dividends before worthless and speculative common stock."[2]

Enough has been said in this very cursory review of well-recognized principles of railway finance, to indicate that the public has a vital interest in restricting the issues, not only of bonds, but also of preferred stocks.

(3) Common Stock

The subject of common stock brings us to the really disputable point in this discussion of the influence of capitalization on credit. With respect to bonds, and even with respect to preferred stock, the wisdom of keeping the issues within safe limits is as generally recognized in theory as it is violated in practice. But with respect to common stock,

---

[1] Daggett finds nine instances of their use in reorganizations since 1907 (*Quarterly Journal of Economics*, vol. xxxii, p. 483).

[2] *Ibid.*, p. 483.

the necessity of any moderate limit has frequently been denied. American corporations, as everyone knows, have been lavish in their issues of this class of security. Even companies that have exercised due restraint with their debts and their preferred stocks, have distributed common stock without stint.

The defense of this financial practice is a plausible one. It rests on the argument that a share of stock is really nothing but a participation certificate. Although nominally it purports to represent a certain *amount* of investment, actually it represents merely a *fractional interest* in the total property, of whatever value that total may be. Par values, therefore, are a pure fiction; they are nothing but a mathematical device for convenient division of the capital into shares. This view of the nature of stock leads to the conclusion that the total par values are a matter of very little consequence. Since the common stock is entitled only to such dividends as may be earned, its amount will have no effect on the burden of capital charges against the issuing company. If the stock be doubled, the rate of dividends may be halved, leaving the total requirements unchanged.

The validity of this argument could hardly be questioned if one were to accept an assumption on which it is based; namely, that dividends on common stock are perfectly flexible. This assumption is indeed true in theory; for common stock carries no fixed rate of dividends but is entitled simply to whatever earnings remain after other charges are provided for. In practice, however, the case is not so simple. Dividend requirements tend to become fixed by the expectations of the investors. If a company is expected to pay dividends at the rate of six per cent, that *expected* rate may become a quasi-fixed charge on the corporate revenues. To be sure, the directors of the company are under no legal obligation to meet that expectation; they may reduce the dividends to four per cent, or they may pass them altogether. But such action can be taken only at the risk of disappointing the stockholders and of creating the feeling that the management has not been as efficient as it should have been. Even if no blame could be attached to the management for failure to earn the dividends, the disappointment would be sure to react unfavorably on the company's credit. Investors could not easily be induced to furnish more capital after former hopes had been disappointed.

For the above reasons, corporate directors are always under pressure to pay the *expected* rate of dividends on common stock. Too often they fail to resist that pressure when the condition of their property demands that all the resources be conserved. The property is starved to meet common stock dividends just as it may be starved to meet the fixed charges.. Examples in point are fairly numerous in the history of American railways. The Erie, in its early career, paid unearned dividends on its excessive stock issues and then falsified the accounts so as to conceal the deficits.[1] Charges of similar practice have been made, unofficially, against the Missouri Pacific[2] and, officially against the Pere Marquette under the Prince management of 1902-4.[3] The Chicago & Eastern Illinois was drained of its resources in order to pay common stock dividends to the Frisco, which had bought the stock at two hundred dollars per share.[4] The New Haven railroad, from 1908 to 1914, paid dividends in excess of its earnings for every year except 1910.[5]

Having in mind this tendency of the *expected* rate of

[1] Daggett, *Railroad Reorganization*, p. 37.

[2] *Moody's Magazine*, vol. xii (1911), p. 319.

[3] 44 I. C. C. Rep. 1 (1917).

[4] 29 I. C. C. Rep. 139 (1914).

[5] The New Haven stock, however, was not watered in the ordinary sense of the term.

dividends to become a quasi-fixed charge, we can now see
that the amount of outstanding common stock is not wholly
a matter of indifference, as so many practical financiers have
maintained. An excessive issue of common stock is
dangerous for the reason that *it tends to create an expectation of excessive dividends.*[1] Stockholders will anticipate larger dividends from a railway company capitalized
at one hundred million dollars than from a precisely similar
property capitalized at only fifty millions. They assume,
for some reason or other, that a higher nominal capitalization
means a higher value and a larger earning capacity.

But why do they make that assumption? To this question there are two possible answers, each of which may be
valid according to circumstances. The one that is usually
given by writers on corporation finance is that the investing
public assumes a correspondence between the par value of a
security and the actual cost or value of the property. While
the shrewd trader may know quite well that par values
are a mere fiction, the innocent " outsider " is thought to be

[1] This statement of the nature of the injury resulting from stock
watering may be compared with a recent discussion of the evil by
Professor Allyn A. Young, presented in Ely's *Outlines of Economics*
(3d rev. ed., New York, 1919, pp. 221-25). Mr. Young writes (p. 223) :
" Overcapitalization always makes available, for example, what may
be termed a surplus of stock, and this surplus, instead of being distributed equally among the different stockholders, may be used in a disproportionate and extravagant payment to the promoter (or organizer)
of the corporation, or the bankers who have assisted in marketing
its securities."
With this statement the present writer is entirely in agreement. Indeed, his own interpretation, as given in the text above, is intended to
supplement Mr. Young's discussion by explaining how a disproportionate allotment of stock to promoters or to bankers may injure, not
merely the bona-fide investors, but also the corporate credit. The injury arises from the fact that the actual investors are not getting as
large a share in the enterprise as they think they are getting; hence,
they will overestimate their dividend prospects, with the untoward
results noted above.

unaware of that fact, or at least only partly aware of it. He assumes, therefore, that a one-hundred-dollar share of stock is worth more than a fifty-dollar share.

That this par-value illusion does, at times, exert some influence, no one familiar with the stock market can seriously doubt. Sufficient proof of this fact is found in the almost universal American practice of overcapitalizing new industrial and railway corporations. Were it not for the possibility of taking advantage of the "magic of par values," corporate promoters would have little or no occasion to indulge in this practice.[1]

It would be a mistake, however, to assume that the deceptive appearance of par values furnishes a complete and sufficient explanation of the curious influence that the nominal amount of capitalization exerts over the market values of the securities. Another factor, even more significant, should not be overlooked. That is the tendency of investors to assume that the value of a share of stock remains unchanged

[1] The writer is aware that this statement may be challenged by those who regard stock watering of new enterprises as having other and more legitimate objects than that of deception. It is sometimes said that bonus stock may be employed simply in order to divide the investor's claim into a fixed claim (for interest) and a contingent claim (for dividends). In that way, it is argued, a bondholder may be induced to accept a lower rate of interest on his bonds than he would have been willing to accept were it not for the stock bonus. This point of view is very ably defended by Hastings Lyon (*Corporation Finance*, Boston, 1916, pt. i, pp. 87-107). But it may be questioned very seriously whether the *mere* desire to divide the claims can account for the use of bonus stock. For that object could be accomplished just as well without the bonus, simply by getting investors to take part of their securities in bonds and part in stock. For example, securities might be offered at par in blocks of four thousand dollars in bonds and one thousand dollars in stock. To be sure, such an offering would probably not sell as readily as would a five thousand dollar bond bearing a lower rate of interest, plus a considerable quantity of bonus stock; but that is precisely because the former offering lacks the *deceptively attractive appearance* of an excessive par value.

even when the total number of shares has been increased. We can best illustrate this point with an example. Suppose that the stock of a certain well-established corporation has been selling at about 150. The company now increases its capitalization by issuing a stock dividend of ten per cent. *Theoretically,* this increase in the number of shares should reduce the value of each share to about 136. *Actually,* however, the market price falls only to, say, 145 and soon may even return to 150. In this case, a particular value has become established in the minds of the investors, so that they fail to discount fully the increased number of shares. But it is the *established* value, rather than the *par* value that is here the influential factor.

Of the two possible sources of deception that we have mentioned,—par value and established value,—one may be active at one time and the other at another time. With new companies, it is the former, rather than the latter, that deludes the investor. But with well-seasoned securities, the situation is reversed. Here the fictitious nature of par values has doubtless already become apparent. Stockholders have already adjusted their valuations on the basis of actual earnings and dividends and have learned to disregard the face values. But let the present capitalization be changed, let the number of shares be increased by the issuance of a stock dividend, and a new danger arises—the danger, namely, that investors will fail properly to discount the increase in the nominal amounts of stock. They will tend to expect the *same rate* of dividends on the *increased number* of shares, with the result that the corporation will be under dangerous pressure to meet this expectation.

The tendency of stocks to maintain their old market values despite an injection of water is a phenomenon well recognized on the stock market. Doubtless this seemingly illogical tendency is due chiefly to the fact, that, in actual experience, corporations have frequently been able to maintain the old rate of dividends even after issuing watered stock. Indeed, the principal purpose of a stock dividend is to permit companies to pay more liberal cash dividends without increasing the nominal dividend rate and without thereby becoming liable to popular attack for profiteering.[1]

It must be admitted that if corporations were to issue stock dividends only when their earnings would safely permit them to maintain the same rate of cash dividends on the higher capitalization, then the practice could hardly be criticized from the point of view of sound finance, however much it might be condemned as an attempt to conceal from the public the true rate of profits. Too often, however, corporations have watered their stock when their earnings have not been sufficent to justify the more liberal dividend policy. In that case, harm has been done, not merely to the private investors who have paid inflated prices for their stock, but also to the credit of the companies, which have suffered under the burden of excessive dividend charges.

Perhaps the two best examples in recent railroad history of the evils of stock watering to which we have alluded are the Alton reorganization in 1899-1900[2] and the Rock Island

---

[1] There is also another reason why an increase in nominal capitalization may cause less than a proportionate decrease in the value of each share: Investors, even though they anticipate a corresponding decrease in the rate of dividends, may prefer to have a larger nominal amount of stock paying a low rate than a smaller amount of stock paying a high rate. The low-dividend stock has the illusory appearance of greater safety. This point was brought out by Professor Bemis in his testimony before the United States Industrial Commission (*Report*, vol. ix, p. 88).

[2] So much dispute has arisen over the facts of the Alton reorganization and over the question as to who was responsible for the company's subsequent misfortunes, that the writer has deemed it necessary to discuss the matter in detail in Appendix C of this study. The subject has much more than a merely historical interest; for it furnishes one of the clearest examples of the evils which governmental regulation of security issues should aim to prevent.

reorganization in 1902.[1] Before its reorganization, each
of these roads was in sound financial condition and was able
to pay reasonable dividends on a conservative capitalization.
Then came the new managements, with policies of expansion and with promises of greatly increased earnings. In
order to enhance the market values of the securities and
thus to sell out at a handsome profit, these controlling interests proceeded by various devices to inflate the capitalization far out of proportion to the increased investment in the
properties. For a short period of time, the increase in the
nominal capitalization caused the market value of the stocks
and bonds to rise far above the old figures.[2] But soon it
became evident that the heavier burden of interest and
dividends was far beyond the ability of the companies to
pay. Then the bubbles burst. The Rock Island, in 1915,
went into the hands of a receiver, and the Alton, its credit
seriously impaired, barely escaped a similar fate owing, it
is said, to the financial support of the Union Pacific.

The position emphasized in the foregoing discussion—
that the source of danger in stock watering lies in the rigidity
of *established* values even more than in the deceptive nature
of *par* values—leads to two conclusions of much practical
consequence. In the first place, it indicates that the evil to
be guarded against is not so much overcapitalization, in the
usual meaning of that term, as an *undiscounted increase* in
capitalization. Indeed, the danger of inflation is almost as

[1] For the facts of the Rock Island case see the special report on this
subject by the Interstate Commerce Commission, 36 I. C. C. Rep. 43
(1915); also, Ripley, *Railroads: Finance and Organization*, p. 524,
et seq.

[2] This same thing had happened once before in the history of the
Rock Island, in 1880, when the company was reorganized so as to increase the share capitalization by about one hundred per cent. This
recapitalization was evidently for the purpose of paying more liberal
dividends without exciting public disfavor. See *Commercial and
Financial Chronicle*, vol. xxx (1880), p. 663.

great in the case of a company that has been *undercapitalized* and that now raises its capitalization to normal as it is in the case of a company which was originally capitalized at its actual cost and which now issues a stock dividend. In the one case, as in the other, investors are liable to be deceived by a false assumption that the increased amount of securities means increased earnings and larger dividends.

The second practical implication of the theory that we have been discussing is that the more serious evils of stock watering cannot be cured by the mere recourse to the recently favored plan of issuing shares without par value. Removal of the par value, to be sure, removes *one* of the sources of deception; but it leaves untouched the other, more potent, source. For, even without par values, an increase in the *number* of shares, unless accompanied by a corresponding increase in earning power. may result in a dangerous inflation of market values.[1]

Stock watering not the only method of inflating market value

Although stock watering is a favorite device by which speculative financiers attempt to inflate market values, it is not the only device. Indeed, unless used in connection with other methods of creating false hopes, it is not apt to be effective. Promoters never rely solely on the tendency of investors to think that more stock means more earnings; they attempt to further that tendency by various kinds of manipulation. Glowing prospectuses and optimistic financial statements are issued; investors are assured that the higher capitalization is justified by the increased earning power that may be expected as a result of the new manage-

---

[1] But this statement is not meant to condemn shares without par value; it is meant simply to indicate their limitations. The matter is discussed at length in Chapter IV, *infra*.

ment, or as a result of the advantages of consolidation with other companies. The deception may be even more downright; it may take the form of falsified earnings statements, "padded" balance sheets, and false rumors of increased dividends.

American railway history can show many examples of these forms of deception, although, in recent years, the situation has been much improved by the strict accounting regulations of the Interstate Commerce Commission. The Erie, in its early days, seriously overstated its earnings in order to pay unearned dividends.[1] The Louisville and Nashville is reported by the Interstate Commerce Commission to have made improper charges on its balance sheet to property account in order to offset the liabilities created by a series of stock dividends issued between 1860 and 1891.[2] More recent cases of misrepresentation have been brought to light by several railway failures occurring within the last few years. Part of the troubles of the Pere Marquette and of the Cincinnati, Hamilton & Dayton was attributed by the Interstate Commerce Commission to an excessive capitalization placed upon the companies in the early part of the present century by a speculative and unscrupulous management. In order to make a market for these securities, interest and dividends were paid out of capital—a fact which was concealed by improper charges to capital account.[3] By similar practices the Rock Island management, under the Reid-Moore control, attempted to give an appearance of reality to a grossly inflated capitalization.[4] The Missouri Pacific, prior to its receivership in 1915, is said to have carried a fictitious surplus for years in order to create the

[1] Daggett, *Railroad Reorganization*, p. 37.
[2] 33 I. C. C. Rep. 168 (1915).
[3] 44 I. C. C. Rep. 1 (1917).
[4] 36 I. C. C. Rep. 43 (1915).

false impression of financial soundness.[1]   Much comment
was caused by a report of the Interstate Commerce Commission on the methods of financing the construction of the
Chicago, Milwaukee & Puget Sound Railway.   This company, in order to circumvent a law of the state of Washington which limited the amount of bonds to twice the amount
of the paid-up capital stock, issued stock in excess of one
hundred million dollars over the cost of the road and then
wrote up the property account in order to conceal the excess.[2]

The fact that stock watering in America has nearly always
been accompanied by other means of misleading the investors, raises the question whether the practice would really
be harmful of itself if only the truth as to actual investment
and actual earnings were not concealed.   Would it not be
sufficient for the government to require the publication of
an accurate statement of investment and of earnings, so
that investors might be in a position fully to discount any
fictitious stock issues?[3]   Several excellent authorities have

[1] " For many years this company has, through carrying a fictitious
surplus, given the impression to the public that it was in sound financial condition, and the policy of paying dividends on the stock for
several years after the time when such dividends should have stopped
still further misrepresented the real situation to the public " (Moody's
Magazine, vol. xii [1911], p. 319).

[2] 29 I. C. C. Rep. 508 (1914).

[3] An eminent authority on accounting, H. R. Hatfield, goes so far
as to say that " the watering of the stock, in itself, aside from ac-
companying complications is the merest peccadillo.   The wrong con-
sists in the ' prevarication,' the positive misstatemment, that among
the assets is a plant worth $100,000 when everyone concerned in the
transactions knows it is worth only $50,000, or the untruth that the
company has acquired Goodwill worth $50,000 when it is absolutely in-
nocent of any such possession.   If the other accounts in the Balance
Sheet are correct little concern need be felt over stock watering.   Its
evil will be slight, its correction automatic." Modern Accounting
(New York, 1913), p. 172.

answered this question in the affirmative.   They have held
that the evil of stock watering is caused, not by the mere presence of the water, but by its *undetected* presence; and they
have argued that what is needed is publicity of the facts
rather than restriction of the stock issue.

We have already had occasion to discuss this point of
view in our study of capitalization as an element in " fair
value" for rate making.[1]   There it was shown that capitalization need not be considered in fixing a value provided
that clear evidence of the actual investment or of the replacement cost is at hand.   May not a similar situation apply
here?   That is, may not investors, like public service commissions, disregard the nominal capitalization as soon as
they are furnished with the proper data for looking *behind*
that capitalization?

To this question only a doubtful answer can be given.   The
doubt arises because of the fact that investors are more ir-
rational in their judgments of value than are rate-making
commissions.   Even though an accurate record of the investment and of the earnings be published, it is doubtful
whether that fact will cause investors to disregard entirely
the par value and the number of their shares, and to discount any increase in that number.   Certainly a full publication of the facts would remove *a large part* of the danger of
deception, but it would be hazardous to say that it would remove *all* danger.

On this point the experience of Great Britain is instruc-
tive.   British railways have been permitted to issue large
quantities of watered stock, but they have been obliged to
show in their balance sheets exactly how much of their stock
represents investment and how much is pure water.   While
this requirement has doubtless prevented the gross forms of
deception that have been practiced by American railways,

[1] *Supra*, pp. 30-31.

it has not been sufficient, in the judgment of some authorities, to remove all misleading appearances.[1]   Indeed, the
very fact that British railways and other public utilities have
issued watered stock in spite of the publicity requirements
is in itself an indication that nominal capitalization still has
a tendency to deceive; for otherwise there could hardly be
any inducement to overcapitalize.[2]

SUMMARY

In the preceding chapter we saw that the chief evil of
overcapitalization lies in its injurious effect on corporate
credit.   The present chapter has therefore discussed the
exact nature of this effect.

Overcapitalization tends to weaken the credit of a railway corporation by creating excessive interest and dividend
charges.   But the amount of these charges is not in direct
proportion to the nominal capitalization.   Much depends on
the nature of the securities.   *Bonds* carry a fixed rate of
interest; they therefore impose a burden of charges that
cannot be lightened in times of adversity.   *Preferred stocks*

---

[1] See Edward R. McDermott, *Railways* (London, 1904), pp. 163-4;
Ching Chun Wang, *Legislative Regulation of Railway Finance in England*
(Urbana, Ill., 1918), 2 pts., pt. ii, pp. 144-6; Lord Monkswell, *The
Railways of Great Britain* (New York, 1914), p. 280.   However, that
any serious injury has resulted from railway stock watering is denied
by W. R. Lawson, *British Railways* (London, 1913), p. 2.   For a
criticism of the similar fictitious increases of capital by the municipal
utilities, see R. H. Whitten, *Regulation of Public Servi   Companies in
Great Britain* (New York, 1914), ch. ii.

[2] This statement may be questioned on the ground that companies may
choose to increase the number of shares so as to reduce the market
value of each share to a figure that is more acceptable for investment
and speculative purposes.   But that object could be attained by increasing the number of shares while at the same time *reducing the par value
to a proportionate extent*, thus leaving the total capitalization just
where it was beforehand.   The fact that this reduction in par value
is not made indicates that the mere convenience of smaller shares is
not the only motive behind a fictitious increase in stock.

also carry a fixed rate, but the dividends may be reduced or completely passed if they are not earned.   Nevertheless, the necessity of passing the preferred dividends reacts unfavorably on the credit of the company; it should therefore be avoided, if possible, by keeping the amount of preferred stock within safe limits.   *Common stock* has no fixed rate of dividends; and this fact has led some financiers to assert that the amount of the issue is a matter of indifference.   But we cannot accept this view.   It fails to take account of the fact that even on common stock the dividends are not perfectly flexible.   Although in theory they are supposed to be determined by actual earnings, in practice they are apt to be held at the *expected* rate.   This rate becomes a quasi-fixed charge, and failure to pay it reacts on the corporate credit in the same way as would the passing of a preferred dividend.   Even more harmful than the *failure* to pay an expected dividend is its *actual payment* out of capital when it has not been earned.   Yet an overcapitalized company is under pressure to do this very thing rather than to admit that it cannot pay its dividends.

But why is it that an excessive issue of stock may cause investors to expect excessive dividends?   Why may they not be content with a lower rate of dividend on the higher amount of stock?   To these questions there are two possible answers.   First, investors may assume that par values represent the actual investment, they will therefore expect the *ordinary* rate of dividends on an *extraordinary* amount of stock.   Second, they may assume that a company which issues watered stock will continue to pay the *established* rate of dividends on the *increased* number of shares.   Of these two points, the second is the more significant.   The danger of stock watering lies therefore not so much in the excess of par value over actual assets as in the increase in the number of shares without a corresponding increase in earning power.

Up to this point, we have discussed the problem of capitalization in its negative aspect: the attempt has been to show the evils that arise from stock watering and other financial abuses. In the remaining chapters we reverse the procedure and consider what principles of capitalization should be followed in order to prevent the recurrence of those evils. The first problem that arises in such a study is the much disputed problem of the basis of capitalization—that is to say, the standard by which to determine the sum total of stocks and bonds which a railway company may properly be allowed to issue. To this question we turn in the following chapter.

CHAPTER III

THE BASIS OF CAPITALIZATION [1]

ACCORDING to a view which, until recently, has gone almost unchallenged, the fundamental principle of capitalization is that the face value of outstanding securities should correspond to the cost, or to the fair value, of the property. As one writer puts it, " presumably the chief purpose of regulation of capitalization is to establish an equilibrium between the capitalization and the bona-fide investment." [2]

[1] For discussions of the basis of capitalization with reference to corporations in general, see Hastings Lyon, *Corporation Finance* (Boston, 1916), pt. i, p. 234, *et seq.*; E. S. Mead, *Corporation Finance* (New York, 1915), ch. xii; Jeremiah Jenks and Walter H. Clark, *The Trust Problem*, rev. ed. (New York, 1917), ch. vii; William H. Lough, *Business Finance* (New York, 1917), ch. viii; William Allen Wood, *Modern Business Corporations*, 2d ed. (Indianapolis, 1917), pp. 32-9; Thomas Conyngton, *Corporate Organization and Management*, 4th ed. (New York, 1918), ch. vii; William Morse Cole, *Accounts: Their Construction and Interpretation* (Boston, 1915), ch. xiii; U. S. Industrial Commission, *Report*, vol. xix (1902), p. 617.

For discussions of the same subject with special reference to railroads and other public utilities, see F. A. Cleveland and F. W. Powell, *Railroad Finance* (New York, 1912), pp. 324-39; Emory R. Johnson and T. W. Van Metre, *Principles of Railroad Transportation* (New York, 1916), pp. 121-24; W. Z. Ripley, *Trusts, Pools and Corporations* (Boston, 1909), ch. vii; U. S. Industrial Commission, *Report*, vol. xix (1902), pp. 408-12. Among the various decisions of public service commissions on security issues, two are especially noteworthy for their discussions of the question of a proper basis of capitalization: Petition of Interstate Consolidated Street Railway Co., 27 Ann. Rep. Mass. R. C. 165 (1895); and *Re* Westchester Street Railroad Co., 3 P. S. C. R. (2d Dist. N. Y.) 286 (1912).

[2] Ralph E. Heilman, " The Development by Commissions of the Principles of Public Utility Capitalization," *Journal of Political Economy*, vol. xxiii (1915), p. 888.

64

Within recent years, however, a new proposal has been made, which is opposed to the orthodox principle of equality between capitalization and assets. Recognizing the difficulties of making par values correspond to actual values, the new plan would abolish par values altogether and thus do away with the possibility of deception which is the chief evil of stock watering. Already the use of stock without par value has been made legal by amendments to the corporation laws of several states and has come into high fashion among industrial corporations. Its possible extension to the interstate railways is certainly worth serious consideration and deserves more attention that it has yet received.

In the following chapter we shall discuss the merits of this new plan as applied to the railways. But before doing so, we must consider the orthodox principle that capitalization should correspond to assets, and we must note the practical difficulties and objections that have led many authorities to favor the abandonment of that principle.

Assuming, then, that there should be an equality between par values and actual assets, the first question to be answered is, On what basis should the assets be valued for the particular purpose at hand? Should the standard be original cost, or reproduction cost, or market value, or some still different measure? This question has given rise to so much controversy that we shall have to discuss it in considerable detail.

At the outset of this inquiry, it is highly important to bear in mind that the problem of a proper basis of capitalization is by no means identical with the more familiar problem of a proper basis of valuation for rate making. To be sure, there is much to be said for the use of the same standard with reference to securities and to rates. But there is also much to be said for *different* standards. To choose but one example of a possible difference: Market value cannot logically be used as a test of the " fair value " of public service property for rate-making purposes, since the market value itself depends on the rates that may be charged.   On the other hand, it can be used with logical consistency as a basis of security issues, since the circular relation no longer applies to the case.   Of course, the determination of a basis of capitalization may depend very largely on the determination of a standard of value for rate making.   But in a discussion of the former topic, the latter problem should be assumed to be settled instead of being discussed.   Emphasis is here laid on the necessity of keeping these two problems distinct, since failure to observe this distinction has led to much confusion in recent discussions of the subject of capitalization.

Most writers on corporation finance have mentioned three possible bases of capitalization: original cost, reproduction cost, and earning capacity.   In an elementary study this threefold classification may be acceptable; but for a more thoroughgoing analysis it is quite inadequate.   Revision as well as enlargement is necessary.   The list that follows is by no means theoretically complete, but it includes at least the more significant standards that have been considered by public service commissions: (1) *rate-making value;* (2) *original investment;* (3) *actual cost (including surplus from reinvested earnings);* (4) *market value;* (5) *earning capacity.*

The reader will note the omission of *reproduction cost* and the substitution for it of *rate-making value.* The purpose of this change is to indicate that no one would propose to base capitalization on the cost of reproduction unless that cost were also to be used in fixing the value for rate making. In the latter event, one might apply the same standard to security issues, not on its own merits, but simply because it corresponds to the rate-making value. Is it not better, therefore, to drop *reproduction cost* from the list of possible bases and to insert in its place *rate-making value?*   We may then consider under this heading the advantages of keeping the basis of capitalization identical with the basis of valuation for rate making, however the latter may be determined; while under the other headings we may discuss the reasons for some independent test of capitalization.

Let us now consider in turn the five possible bases mentioned above, first noting the opinions of various public service commissions and then summarizing the arguments for and against each basis.

(1) Rate-making Value

At first glance, it would seem fairly obvious that the par value of outstanding securities should correspond to the value of the property for rate-making purposes.   Such a conformity would serve to inform investors as to the return which they might be permitted to earn.   Yet nearly all public service commissions have seen fit to make a distinction between a fair value for rates and a standard for security issues.

To this general statement, however, some exceptions must be noted.   The example of Maryland is a case in point. Several years ago, the Public Service Commission of that state made a report to the legislature, in which it complained that it was not permitted, under the law as it then stood, to authorize the issuance of stock dividends.   To this restriction the commission objected on the ground that stock dividends are a necessary means of adjusting capitalization to value for rate making.   The report said:

But in a case where the books have been accurately kept, no disadvantage could accrue to the public by permitting the capitalization of earnings expended in plant extensions for a period of, say, five years before the application.   So far as rate making is concerned, it is based, under the rulings of the courts, upon the value of the property, and the more nearly the value of the property and the par value of the outstanding securities agree, the less likelihood there is of misunderstanding upon the part of the public, and the less difficulty the commission will have in administering the law justly and to the best advantage of all concerned.[1]

Apparently this report of the commission was heeded by the legislature, for in 1918 the public service law was amended so as to permit corporations under its jurisdiction to issue securities

when necessary or desirable, in the discretion of the commission, to cause the aggregate capitalization to conform to the fair value of the property of such corporations as established by the commission pursuant to the provision of section 30 of this Act.[2]

" Fair value " in the above statute means value for rate-making purposes. The law does not state how it is to be measured, but the commission has used a composite of factors without accepting any one basis as alone controlling.[3]

The New York Public Service Commission for the First District, while not accepting consistently any one basis of capitalization, has several times indicated that the same standard should be used for securities as for rate-making value. In the decision on the Second Reorganization Plan of the Third Avenue Railway Company, rejecting the plea that securities should be approved to an amount equal to

[1] 4 Ann. Rep. Md. P. S. C. 21 (1913), P. U. R. 1917 D 857.

[2] L. 1918, ch. 408, sec. 27.

[3] See, for example, the rate case, *Re* Chesapeake & Potomac Telephone Co., P. U. R. 1916 C 925. In at least one case the commission has already authorized a security issue under the provision of the amendment of 1918 (*Re* Chesapeake & Potomac Telephone Co., 9 Ann. Rep. Md. P. S. C. 286 [1918], abstracted in P. U. R. 1919 A 1026).

the original investment, Commissioner Maltbie delivered
the following opinion:

The mere fact of investment does not establish a perpetual
value not only because a mistake in judgment may be made,
but also because property may be allowed to deteriorate, because progress in the arts may make it obsolete, and because
a change in economic conditions may decrease the use made
of it by the public. . . . The commission believes the proposition to be sound that capitalization should have a direct relation to value.[1]

By " value " the commissioner appears here to mean replacement cost depreciated.   It is clear that the decision is applying to capitalization the same tests that would be applied
in finding the " fair value " in a rate case.   To be sure, the
commission has more recently expressed a preference for
actual cost rather than replacement cost as a basis for security issues. whenever that cost can be ascertained.[2]   But
this preference does not indicate a distinction between the
basis of capitalization and that of rate-making value, since
the commission, in its more recent decisions, has been inclined
to accept actual cost for the latter purpose as well as for
the former.[3]

The California Railroad Commission, on at least one occasion, has accepted by implication the view that rate-making
value, based on replacement cost depreciated, should also be

[1] 2 P. S. C. R. (1st Dist. N. Y.) 390 (1910).

[2] *Re* Bronx Gas & Elec. Co., 6 P. S. C. R. (1st Dist. N. Y.) 243 (1915).
In approving the issuance of securities to purchase new property the
commission has always used actual cost as the test; see the list of
precedents cited in Manhattan & Queens Traction Corporation, 5 P. S.
C. R. (1st Dist. N. Y.) 71 (1914).

[3] See, for example, *Re* N. Y. & North Shore Traction Co., P. U. R.
1918 A 893; also, Maires *v.* Flatbush Gas Co., *N. Y. State Dept. Repts.*,
vol. xv (1918), p. 171.

the standard of capitalization. In an application of the
Pacific Gas and Electric Company for permission to issue a
stock dividend, the commission denied the petition on the
ground that the dividend would create a disparity between
the total amount of securities outstanding and the replacement cost depreciated.[1]

But the opinions cited above are exceptional. The more
general practice is to use different tests for security issues
and for rate-making value. The prevailing tendency is to
authorize security issues on the basis of original investment
or actual cost, while using cost of reproduction at least as
one of the important factors in fixing the " fair value " on
which to base rates. In the following section we shall discuss the reasons for this policy.

Other distinctions have also been made. In a recent reorganization case, the Missouri Public Service Commission
gave two possible reasons for differentiation. The opinion
reads as follows :

The determination of fair value for the purpose of limiting
the securities to be issued on reorganization of a railroad company is a different question from determining present value
in a rate case, in at least one respect, that the " earning power
at reasonable rates " is to be taken into consideration in the
former. There may also be property not used and useful for
railroad purposes which might properly be included in determination of value of property in a reorganization, and
excluded in a valuation for rate making.[2]

The first distinction in the above-quoted opinion, by
which earning power is considered in capitalization cases
though not in rate cases, has also been maintained by the
New York Commission for the Second District and by other

[1] P. U. R. 1916 D 276.
[2] *Re* St. L. & S. F. R. R. Co., 3 Mo. P. S. C. 664, 689, P. U. R. 1916
F 77.   See also *Re* Dunham, P. U. R. 1916 E 544.

rate-making bodies; to these cases reference will be made in the section on the market-value basis.

The second distinction, according to which certain property may be included in the value for capitalization but not in the value for rates, is due to the fact that railroads engage to a greater or less extent in outside business. Non-railroad property may not be included in valuation for rate making, but if it is recognized as a legitimate undertaking for a railroad, it may be considered in the capitalization allowance.[1]

Still another divergence between rate-value and capitalization-value was indicated by the New York Court of Appeals, in a review of a rate decision by the Public Service Commission for the First District.[2] The case involved the treatment of " going-value " in the Wisconsin sense of the accrued deficit from early operation. The commission, in opposing the allowance of this item in rate-value, argued that such deficits are not properly subjects of capitalization. To this contention the court replied as follows:

It may be, as is urged, that a well-conducted enterprise will charge the cost of developing the business to operating expenses and that it would open the door to an overissue of securities to permit the capitalization of early losses. In answer, it is sufficient to say that we are dealing, not with proper methods of bookkeeping, not with the proper capitalization upon which to issue securities, but solely with the fair return which the company is entitled to receive from the public. Treating a reasonably necessary and proper outlay in building up a business as an investment for the purpose of determining the fair rate of return to be charged is far from hold-

---

[1] On this point see D. & H. Co., 1 P. S. C. R. (2nd Dist. N. Y.) 392 (1908), decision reversed in People *ex rel.*, the D. & H. Co. *v.* Stevens, 197 N. Y. 1.

[2] Kings County Lighting Co. *v.* Willcox, 210 N. Y. 479 (1914).

ing that it should be treated as capital against which securities might be issued.[1]

Accrued deficits, according to this decision, may properly be added to rate value, but perhaps not properly added to capitalization. The court did not state the grounds on which it made this distinction, but one may surmise that it had in mind the prudence of valuing and capitalizing corporate assets at a minimum.

Summing up these various opinions of courts and commissions, one finds sanction for each of the following distinctions between the basis of capitalization and the basis of rate-making value: (1) the use of original investment or actual cost in the former case and replacement cost in the latter; (2) the acceptance of earning capacity as a factor in the one case but not in the other; (3) the addition of the value of non-public-service property for securities but not for rates; (4) the allowance of accrued deficits from early operation as an item in rate-making value but the rejection of this item in fixing the proper capitalization. Doubtless other distinctions have been made which have not come to the writer's attention.[2]

What, now, is to be said for the use of the same standard of value in security cases as in rate cases, and why have commissions so generally adopted different bases? The chief reason for accepting the same basis has already been suggested: It is that the par value of securities is ac-

[1] *Ibid.*, pp. 488-9.

[2] The tendency of nearly all commissions is to be much more liberal in fixing the limit for security issues than in setting a value for rate making. For example, most commissions have on occasion permitted the capitalization of replacements, and some of them have authorized the issuance of securities below par. But action of this sort has been a concession to the necessities of the case, taken by commissions with the full recognition of the fact that it violates the accepted principles of sound capitalization. On this point, see pp. 93-95, *infra*.

cepted by the unwary as an indication of the actual value, and therefore that any excess of capitalization over value for rate making might deceive investors as to the return that they would be permitted to earn. Of course, such a danger would not be present if the amount of securities were less than the valuation for rate making; and precisely that situation might be expected in most cases at the present time, where securities are based on original cost, while rates are based on cost of replacement. But original cost is not in all cases less than replacement cost; and in the future, under a period of falling prices, the tendency may be quite the reverse.

In spite of this cogent reason in favor of the same standard for securities as for rates, the argument against it is even stronger, as long as rates are to be based on cost of replacement. One objection alone would be conclusive against basing securities on the latter standard; namely, the practical difficulty of reducing outstanding capitalization in order to make it correspond to a fall in the value of the property. Once the securities are issued, they cannot be recalled except at great inconvenience to the holders. Moreover, legal difficulties might prevent a scaling-down. On that account, it is essential that the basis for security issues be stable, not subject to fluctuations with changing physical valuations of the property.

But even if the practical objections to the use of replacement cost could be overcome, the wisdom of applying that standard to security issues would be very doubtful. On many accounts it is important that the par value of the securities should represent the actual investment, even though some other test of " fair value " for rate making be accepted. This point is discussed in the following section.

(2) Original Investment

According to this basis, every dollar in par value of stocks and bonds must represent a dollar contributed to the enterprise by the investors. No securities may be issued to cover unearned increment, and none may be issued against surplus from reinvested earnings.

On the whole, one may say that those commissions which do not permit the use of stock dividends accept original investment as the proper basis of capitalization; for obviously, if some other standard, such as replacement cost or market value, were adopted, it would be necessary to authorize stock dividends whenever the valuation should exceed the amount of outstanding securities.[1] In Massachusetts, New Hampshire, South Carolina, and the District of Columbia, stock dividends are illegal,[2] while in other states their use is much restricted by commission rulings.

For many years the policy of Massachusetts has been to limit stock and bond issues of public utilities to the original investment.[3] Every application by companies for permission to capitalize their surplus has been denied by the regulating commissions. This drastic restriction of security issues is in large measure the outcome of principles of rate regulation that have been accepted in Massachusetts—at least in the case of gas and electric companies. The Board of

[1] This statement is subject to qualification. For instance, in reorganization cases and in consolidation cases the new capitalization may be made to correspond to replacement cost or to any other basis without resort to the use of a stock dividend in the technical sense of the term. The practice of commissions in reorganization cases is noted below, pp. 88-89.

[3] Mary L. Barron, "State Regulation of the Securities of Railroads and Public Service Companies," *Annals of the American Academy of Political and Social Science*, vol. lxxvi (1918), p. 181.

[2] This policy, however, is not in every respect consistently followed; exceptions are noted at a later point in this chapter, pp. 89-90.

Gas and Electric Light Commissioners of that state has always denied the right of utilities to earn on their surplus such high rates of profit as are allowed on the capital contributed by the investors. Quite naturally, therefore, it has refused to permit the issuance of securities against surplus; for such permission would appear to concede the right of stockholders to earn the normal rate of return on the entire property.[1]

In the matter of security issues, New Hampshire has followed the Massachusetts precedent by forbidding stock dividends.[2] But unlike Massachusetts, the New Hampshire Public Service Commission has not accepted original investment as the controlling basis in a rate case.[3] Here, then, is another illustration of the tendency of commissions

[1] Cases illustrating the position of the Massachusetts Board of Gas and Electric Light Commissioners in the matter of surplus are:

(a) With respect to rate making, Springfield Gas Co., 9 Ann. Rep. 6 (1893); East Boston Gas Co., *ibid.*, p. 9; Worcester Gas Lt. Co., 10 Ann. Rep. 31 (1894); Haverhill Gas Co., 16 Ann. Rep. 9 (1900); Haverhill Gas Co., 28 Ann. Rep. 41 (1912). *Cf.* also an article by Morris Schaff, Chairman of the Mass. Board of Gas and Electric Light Commissioners, on " Capitalization of Earnings of Public Service Companies," *Annals Amer. Acad. Pol. & Soc. Science*, vol. liii (May, 1914), pp. 178-181.

(b) With respect to security issues, Edison Elec. Illum. Co. of Fall River, 11 Ann. Rep. 20 (1895); Malden & Melrose Gas Lt. Co., *ibid.*, p. 29; Haverhill Gas Securities Co., 15 Ann. Rep. 6 (1899) and 16 Ann. Rep. 11 (1900); Haverhill Gas Co., 27 Ann. Rep. 79 (1911); Fall River Gas Works Co., 28 Ann. Rep. 98, reversed by court in 214 Mass. 529.

[2] See, for example, Grafton County Elec. Lt. & P. Co., 5 N. H. P. S. C. R. 160. In this case, the commission went so far as to refuse to permit a merger on the ground that it would result in an increase of capitalization and would therefore violate the spirit of the law forbidding stock dividends. This decision, however, was overruled by the court (Grafton County Elec. Lt. & P. Co. *v.* State, 77 N. H. 539, 94 Atl. 193, P. U. R. 1915 C (1064).

[3] In rate cases this commission has refused to accept exclusively any one basis of valuation, but has assumed to consider all relevant factors. See the Index-Digests in vols. iv and vi of its *Reports.*

to distinguish between the " fair value " for rate making and
the basis of capitalization.

Let us now consider the merits of original investment
as the standard in security cases.   Of course, its advantages
would be clear enough if rate-making value were to be
determined by the same method.   But, with the important
exception of Massachusetts, public service commissions have
followed the rulings of courts in refusing to accept that
basis in rate cases.   On what grounds, then, may it be used
as the basis of capitalization?

To this question the answer is two-fold.   In the first
place, the original investment basis has the practical merit of
being stable, whereas most other bases are fluctuating.   We
have already noted this point as a fatal objection to the use
of replacement cost.   In the second place, there is a decided
advantage in making the par value of the securities stand as
a public record of the actual contribution of investors.
Even though this contribution may not be used at the present time as the criterion of " fair value " in rate regulation,
it should nevertheless be given all possible publicity.
Finality in the principles of valuation has been by no means
attained; and it is quite possible that publicity of the actual
investment, if it should reveal excessive rates of profit,
might lead to a radical revision of the present methods of
valuation.   But even assuming reproduction cost to be the
permanent method of valuation in rate cases, it is highly
important that investors should know the actual rates of
profit on the original investment.   Those who support the
use of replacement cost as the basis of valuation say that
the possibilty of gain through unearned increment in the
values of land and other fixed capital will serve as an inducement to investors in lieu of a higher rate of return on the
original contribution.   But this view presupposes not
merely the possibility of unearned increment but also the

recognition of that possibility by investors. The best way to advertise the opportunity for future profits is to make known the actual gains in the past; and for that purpose a capitalization restricted to the original investment would be most effective.

(3) Actual Cost

This standard resembles the previous one in using original rather than present cost but differs from it in taking the cost of the *entire property*—not merely that part of the cost that was defrayed from the proceeds of security issues. In a word, the difference is this: that actual cost equals original investment plus surplus from reinvested earnings.

Of the many disputable points of rate regulation, few have given the courts and commissions more concern than the treatment of corporate surplus in fixing a "fair value." Is a public service company entitled to a return on the earnings that have been reinvested in the property, or should it be restricted to a fair return on the original contribution? To this question commissions have given different answers, although courts have almost invariably held that a return may be earned on surplus. We are not here concerned, however, with the merits of this controversy. That is a problem in rate making and not a question of capitalization. For us the problem is simply this: Assuming that a company *is* entitled to a return on surplus from reinvested earnings, should it also be permitted to capitalize this surplus by issuing certificates against it?

As we have already noted, public service commissions have to face this problem in connection with applications for permission to issue stock dividends. Such issues are justified by applicants on the ground that they represent actual capital secured by the reinvestment of earnings which might have been distributed among stockholders in the form of a cash dividend. On this point the laws and practices of the different states vary. We have already observed that Massachusetts and New Hampshire strictly forbid stock dividends. On the other hand, the commissions of New Jersey,[1] Vermont,[2] Michigan,[2] Ohio,[2] Illinois,[3] Indiana [4] and California [5] have authorized companies to issue stock dividends in order to capitalize a bona-fide surplus from reinvested earnings. Where this practice has been permitted, the actual cost basis of capitalization is generally the accepted principle.[6]

Even some commissions that do not directly permit the use of stock dividends have allowed the same end to be attained by indirect means. In this matter the precedent has been set by New York. Up to 1910, the law of that state provided that a public service corporation might issue securities only for one of the following purposes: (1) the acquisition of property; (2) the construction, completion, extension or improvement of its facilities; (3) the improvement or maintenance of its service; and (4) the discharge or lawful re-

[1] P. U. R. 1917 E 720, 1918 B 240 and 1046. See also a statement by the New Jersey commission of general principles governing its action in security cases, 3 Ann. Rep. N. J. P. U. C. 161 (1912).

[2] P. U. R. 1916 C 606, 607.

[3] P. U. R. 1915 A 205.

[4] P. U. R. 1915 A 540.

[5] P. U. R. 1915 C 324, 1916 D 276.

[6] It would not be correct, however, to say that *all* commissions which permit stock dividends accept the actual cost basis of capitalization. For example, the Maryland Public Service Commission is authorized by law to permit stock dividends when necessary to make the total capitalization equal " fair value," *i. e.*, rate-making value. The California commission on one occasion refused to permit the issuance of a stock dividend on the ground that capitalization would thereby be raised above the rate-making value. Both of these cases have been noted above, under the heading, *Rate-making Value*. But these are exceptional cases.

funding of its obligations.[1] These four conditions, which
were copied almost verbatim by other states,[2] did not seem
to authorize security issues for the purpose of capitalizing
reinvested earnings—at least, so it was held by the New
York Commission for the Second District.[3] But in 1910
the law was amended and a fifth clause added, which provides that securities may be issued " for the reimbursement
of moneys actually expended from income or from any
other moneys in the treasury of the corporation . . . within
five years next prior to the filing of an application with the
proper commission."[4] This new clause, which was soon
copied by other states,[5] entitles a company that has reinvested earnings in its property to capitalize the resulting
surplus by issuing new securities. Whether or not the
amendment directly permits stock dividends is a point on
which commissions have differed. The California Railroad Commission seems to have answered in the affirmative.[6]
On the other hand, the New York Public Service Commis-

[1] L. 1907, ch. 429, secs. 55 and 69.

[2] Several states still retain these four conditions without the amendment presently to be noted. According to my latest information,
these states are Georgia, Kansas, Massachusetts, Michigan, Nebraska,
and New Hampshire.

[3] *Re* Erie R. R. Co., 1 P. S. C. R. (N. Y. 2nd Dist.) 115 (1908);
Re Babylon Elec. Lt. Co., *ibid.*, p. 132. On the other hand, the Georgia
Railroad Commission, acting on the advice of counsel, held that it was
empowered to permit stock dividends under a law similar to that of
New York (38 Ann. Rep. Ga. R. C. 31, 93 [1910]). Perhaps, however, the Georgia commission may have based its decision on a clause
in the statute, not present in the New York law, stating as a fifth
condition that securities may be issued " for lawful corporate purposes
falling within the spirit of this provision."

[4] L. 1910, ch. 480, secs. 55 and 69.

[5] Arizona, California, Illinois, Indiana, Maine, Missouri, Ohio, Wisconsin (Barron, *op. cit.*, p. 179).

[6] P. U. R. 1915 C 324, 1916 D 276.

sion for the Second District does not interpret the amendment of 1910 as sanctioning stock dividends. It holds that, under the fifth clause, securities may be issued only for cash, and that this cash must be used to " reimburse the treasury " for funds that it has already paid out on capital account.[1] But whichever way the law is interpreted, the practical result may be the same. For a company, under the New York ruling, may simply issue stock for cash, and may immediately afterwards pay out that cash in dividends. As the New York commission seems to have recognized,[2] the outcome in this case would be precisely the same as if the company had issued a stock dividend.[3]

At the present time, actual cost is by far the most widely accepted basis of capitalization among state commissions.

[1] *Re* Central Hudson Gas & Elec. Co., 3 P. S. C. R. (2nd Dist. N. Y.) 386 (1912).

[2] *Ibid.*

[3] To the above statement, which the writer published in substantially the same form in a recent article (*Pol. Sci. Quart.*, vol. xxxv [1920], p. 43), exception is taken by Mr. Ledyard P. Hale, Counsel for the New York Public Service Commission, Second District. In a personal letter Mr. Hale writes: " There is a substantial difference between a stock dividend and the temporary use for capitalization expenditures of a surplus which might be paid out in dividends when so used but which in fact is not paid out then but later. As administered by the commission, the Amendment of 1910 simply puts ordinary small expenditures for capital purposes within the business judgment and discretion of directors and avoids applying to the commission every time such a small matter is contemplated."

The present writer is quite ready to accept Mr. Hale's statement that, in actual experience, the law has not yet been used as a means of capitalizing large surpluses and to concede that therefore the law has not *yet* proved to be a means of evading the prohibition of stock dividends. But the possibility of evasion remains. Is it not probable that the failure of companies hitherto to capitalize anything more than "ordinary small expenditures" has been due to their failure to earn any large surpluses during recent years? And will not the situation be different in the future in the event of a return of prosperity to the public service industries?

What accounts for its general acceptance? Compared to rate-making value—as that value is usually determined—it has the marked advantage of being stable. But, as we have already observed, this merit is also possessed by the original investment basis. Why, then, should actual cost be preferred to the latter standard? In other words, why should surplus be capitalized? To this question an obvious reply would be that, since surplus, under the rulings of the courts, must be counted as part of the property on which investors may claim a return, there is no need to distinguish it from any other part of the investment by leaving it uncapitalized. But that statement may be seriously questioned. At least two reasons may be given for making the distinction between surplus and original capital. In the first place, it is sound financial policy to maintain a surplus as a reserve to equalize dividends over good and bad years and to meet emergency demands.[1] In the second place, it is important to keep a record of the amount of capital contributed by investors as distinct from the amount contributed in earnings by the rate-paying public. What the public wants to know, and what the investors need to know, is the exact relation between the net earnings of a public utility and the contribution of the security holders. This relation can be most clearly seen if the outstanding securities represent, dollar for dollar, the original investment. We have already discussed this point in the previous section.

In view of these serious objections to the capitalization

[1] However, it would not always be necessary to devote the entire surplus to that purpose; a sufficient part might be set aside as a reserve. and the remainder capitalized. Indeed, this compromise measure has been approved by the New Jersey Board of Public Utility Commissioners in a recent security case, in which it allowed a company to issue stock dividends, but required it to leave uncapitalized fifteen per cent of the cost of the property (Toms River Elec. Co., 5 Ann. Rep. N. J. P. U. C. 682 [1918]).

of surplus, why do most states permit the practice? Probably this liberality is due not so much to theoretical principles as to practical considerations of finance. Many public utilities would be unwilling to reinvest earnings in improvements if they were not given the opportunity to capitalize that reinvestment by issuing stock dividends. Therefore in order to induce companies to make improvements out of earnings, commissions have adopted the liberal policy with respect to securities. Whether or not the advantages to be secured by this concession outweigh the disadvantages of concealing the original investment—and hence, the actual rate of profits—is a question which the writer does not attempt to answer. But he would call attention to the fact that the Railroad Securities Commission, in its now famous report to the President, expressed the view that all stock and scrip dividends should be prohibited. "It is far better," said the report, "to let the increased value be shown by a higher rate of dividend on the existing shares of stock, instead of by an addition to their nominal amount." [1]

(4) and (5) Market Value and Earning Capacity

According to the market value basis, securities should be issued in such amounts as to make the total par values approximately equal to the market values. All stocks and all bonds must be worth par, or else those which are quoted below par must be offset by those which are quoted at a premium.

Writers on corporation finance have often failed to distinguish between the market-value basis and a kindred but by no means identical basis, usually termed " earning capacity " or " earning power." As the term is currently used, it means simply the expected net earnings capitalized at some hypothetical rate of interest—say four or five per cent. The

[1] *Report of the Railroad Securities Commission*, p. 27.

figure arrived at by this mathematical process is supposed to indicate the proper limit of security issues. Obviously, a capitalization arrived at in this manner may have some relaton to the market values of the securities, for these values depend to a very large extent upon the net earnings. But, although the two bases are related, they may differ widely in amount. Everything depends on the rates of capitalization. If "earning power" happens to be computed at the same rate at which the market capitalizes the earnings, it will be identical with market value—otherwise not.

For the most part, commissions have sanctioned neither market value nor earning capacity as the test of proper capitalization. But to this rule there have been exceptions. The public utilities statutes of New York and of Missouri recognize "earning power at reasonable rates" as one of the elements to be considered in determining the " fair structural value " for capitalization in reorganization cases.[1] A more unqualified endorsement of the earning-power theory was given ir some early decisions of the New York Public Service Commission for the Second District. In an opinion on the application of the Westchester Street Railroad Company [2] for permission to issue capital stock, Chairman Stevens discussed at length the proper basis of capitalization. After remarking that value, in the strict economic sense of the word, means nothing but exchange value, he concluded:

In cases where the sole attraction of a property which gives it exchange value, or in other words creates a desire for its ownership, is pecuniary gain, the measure of the desire and hence of the ratio of exchange is clearly the amount of gain which it is believed can be realized. The fundamental consideration indicates that the net earnings rule of valuation,

---

[1] This point is discussed further on pp. 88-89, *infra*.

[2] 3 P. S. C. R. (2nd Dist. N. Y.) 286 (1912); decision reversed, 158 App. Div. (N. Y.) 251, modified, 210 N. Y. 456, 211 N. Y. 533.

when properly and carefully applied with due regard to all the features of the individual case, is probably the one having the surest support of basic principles.[1]

In the case at hand, the company had failed to earn even operating expenses, but the commission allowed a capitalization of about $400,000, perhaps as a generous estimate of the earning possibilities for the future.   That figure was below the estimated replacement cost depreciated—$445,694; so that, in this particular instance, earning power was the conservative rather than the liberal basis.   This ruling of the New York commission, however, was not unanimous. In an able dissenting opinion Commissioner Sague said:

I disagree with the theory as developed in this case, and believe that too much stress is placed upon the element of earning power, and too little on the other items which determine value . . . the duty of the commission is to approve of an amount of capital which can be used in making up an honest balance sheet which can be applied later, either by the commission or the public, as a basis for determining whether a corporation is giving its customers fair treatment . . . the most important basis for capitalization would appear to be the money which has been skilfully and economically invested in the property.[2]

A similar majority decision and a similar dissenting opinion from Commissioner Sague were rendered on the application of the Canadian American Power Corporation[3] for permission to capitalize a profitable contract for the purchase of electricity.

The Illinois Public Service Commission has also given weight to earning power in certain security cases. In several

[1] *Ibid.*, 327.
[2] *Ibid.*, 342.
[3] 4 P. S. C. R. (2nd Dist. N. Y.) 40 (1914).

instances the commission has permitted a company to purchase property, and to capitalize that purchase, at an amount in excess of the fair value for rate-making purposes.[1] This distinction was justified, in one case, in the following words:

This commission, among others, has heretofore recognized the difference between the value of a utility when used as a basis for fixing schedules of rates and when it is made the object of purchase and sale between a willing buyer and seller. The allowance of the higher value in the latter case may easily be justified upon the grounds that a prospective purchaser may be satisfied with a smaller return upon his money than he may believe the commission would allow him in a possible future rate-making inquiry . . .[2]

Much the same position was taken by the New Hampshire Supreme Court in overruling a decision of the New Hampshire Public Service Commission, which had refused to allow a desired increase of securities upon consolidation.[3] The decision turned partly on the question whether such an increase violated the law forbidding stock dividends and partly on the more general question of the propriety of the proposed capitalization. On both points the commission had decided against the company; but on both points this decision was overruled by the court. According to the court, the value of the property for the purpose of issuing securities should be based on the answer to the question, " What would a single individual, with abundant means, desirous of engaging in the business, but perhaps cautious in making investments, pay for such properties in the situation found upon the data of the capitalization?"[4] Here the

[1] *Re* Ill. Termin. R. Co., P. U. R. 1917 B 494; *cf.* also 4 Ill. P. U. C. 850, 855, 859 (1917).

[2] P. U. R. 1917 B 509-10.

[3] Grafton County Elec. L. & P. Co. *v.* State, 78 N. H. 330, 100 Atl. 668, P. U. R. 1917 E 345; *cf.* also P. U. R. 1915 C 1064.

[4] P. U. R. 1917 E 348.

court apparently accepts "reasonable market value" as the basis for security issues.

The principal argument usually advanced in support of both the market-value and the earning-capacity bases of capitalization rests on the appeal to so-called sound economic theory. Capitalization, it is said, should represent the value of the property. But value, in its strict economic sense, means simply *market* value. Therefore the popular notion that capitalization should be equal to cost,—whether original cost or replacement cost,—rests on an economic fallacy. The proper standard is either market value or earning power, which is the basis of market value.

If the above appeal to "sound economics" could be accepted as having any claim whatever to validity, it would apply only to the strict market-value basis of capitalization and not to the earning-power basis. For current economic theory recognizes no capitalization of earnings at any other rate than the actual market rate. The idea of finding value by capitalizing net earnings at an assumed rate is quite foreign to economic theory.

But irrespective of this point, the argument rests on an invalid assumption; it assumes that capitalization should really be based on value, and that the only problem is to determine what that value is. As a matter of fact, the very opposite is more nearly true. Capitalization might better represent almost any other significant fact than value. For the value may be found simply by reference to current price quotations. Why, then, attempt to indicate it in the par values? The same remark is in point with respect to the earning-power basis. As Cole puts it,

What is the advantage of capitalizing on the basis of earning capacity? . . . The mere schoolboy, if you tell him the earnings of a company, and the rate of interest, can tell you its capitalized value. In other words, to register on the books a capitalization based on earning capacity is not only to register an unnecessary figure, but to bury the actual cost of the assets.[1]

The real grounds, however, upon which the earning-power basis is favored by most financiers are quite different from the theoretical reasons stated above. Securities may be made more marketable if the capitalization is in more or less direct relation to the net earnings. A small issue of stock, paying high rates of dividends, cannot be sold on such favorable terms as can a larger issue that pays the same *amount* of dividends but at lower nominal *rates*. Investors feel that a stock paying only four per cent is safer than a stock paying eight of ten per cent, and therefore they will pay more in proportion for the former.

The earning-power basis of capitalization allows financiers to take advantage of this preference for low-dividend-paying stocks. By making a very liberal and optimistic estimate of the future earnings and by capitalizing this estimate at a high amount,—that is, at a low rate,—they are able to raise market values above the prices that would prevail under a more conservative capitalization.

But when the earning-capacity basis is interpreted and justified in this way, it loses all pretense of representing the value of the property. Capitalization, instead of corresponding to the assets, is really determined at whatever amount will give to the securities their highest market values. The principle was aptly stated by Frederick Strauss when he remarked that " capital seeks that form of expression in the way of stock and bond issues that has the greatest market value." [2] Since this principle is at the root of all those evils of stock watering that we desire to prevent, it

[1] William Morse Cole, *Accounts, Their Construction and Interpretation*, rev. ed. (Boston, 1915), p. 208.

[2] *Public Service Magazine*, vol. xiv (1913), p. 99.

will hardly be accepted in defense of earning power as the proper basis of capitalization.

Conflicting Practices of Commissions

Assuming the validity of the principle that nominal capitalization should correspond to actual assets, which of the five proposed bases of valuation should be chosen? In principle, at least, the choice should rest with that basis which will be most useful as a public record. Judged by this test, market value, earning capacity, and perhaps even rate-making value would have to be ruled out—market value because it is easily noted from the stock quotations; earning capacity because it can be computed by anyone who knows the net earnings and the assumed rate of capitalization; rate-making value because it is given so much publicity in rate decisions that some different statistical fact might better be represented in the nominal capitalization. The choice, then, would seem to lie between original investment and actual cost, with the balance in favor of the former.

This, we say, would be the logical choice. But in practice, public service commissions have followed no such line of reasoning. They have used first one basis, then another, then a combination of several—depending on the circumstances of the particular case.

In reorganization cases, especially, one finds the greatest lack of uniformity. For this indefiniteness the state laws are largely responsible. Illinois, for instance, makes the vague requirement that the capitalization of reorganized companies must not exceed the " fair value." [1] Wisconsin places the limit at the "true value." [2] Still more confusing is the New York law,[3] copied almost verbatim by Missouri. It reads as follows

[1] Stats. (1913-16), ch. 111ᵃ, par. 8686 (37).
[2] Stats. (1919), ch. 85, sec. 1753 (11).
[3] Public Service Commissions Law, secs. 55a and 69a.

Upon all such reorganizations the amount of capitalization
. . . shall be such as is authorized by the commission which,
in making its determination, shall not exceed the fair value
of the property involved, taking into consideration its original
cost of construction, duplication cost, present condition, earning power at reasonable rates and all other relevant matters
and any additional sum or sums as shall be actually paid in
cash, provided, however, that the commission may make due
allowance for discount of bonds.

This long enumeration of elements to be considered in
determining capitalization has the effect of preventing any
approach to a definite standard.   By proper jugglery of the
various factors almost any capitalization may be justified
as conforming to " fair value."   That such is the outcome
in practice is indicated by the recent decisions of the Missouri Public Service Commission, which has been called upon
to approve two very important reorganizations under the
requirements of a statute similar to that of New York.[1]
One looks in vain in these decisions for any scientific basis
upon which the various amounts allowed were held to
indicate " fair value."

Another striking example of the conflict between different
principles of capitalization is to be found in the practice of
Massachusetts.   The commissions of that state are on record as supporting the original-investment basis of capitalization.   According to the Public Service Commission, " the
general purpose of the so called ' anti-stock-watering laws '
is to limit capitalization to honest and reasonable investment, dollar for dollar."[2]   At another time it said, " our
whole anti-stock-watering public utility code rests on the

[1] Re St. Louis & S. F. R. Co., December 22, 1915, P. U. R. 1916 F 49;
Re Dunham [reorganization of Kansas City street railways], December
28, 1915, P. U. R. 1916 E 544.
[2] Bay State Rate Case, 4 Mass. P. S. C. 33 (1916).

assumption that rates are to be mainly determined by figuring a fair return on capital [*i. e.,* capitalization] and that therefore capital should accurately represent investment, no less no more." [1]   Yet, in two important respects this rule is violated.   In the first place, it is violated by the law that the capitalization of reorganized street-railway companies shall not exceed the " fair cost of replacement." [2]   In the second place, it is violated by the requirement that stock must be sold at a price not materially below its market value, even when that price is above par. [3]

Attention has already been called to the conflicting practices of the New York commissions.   At least four out of the five proposed bases of capitalization have been applied by them at various times.   Original investment seems to be the standard implied in the law forbidding the issuance of stock dividends.   But the commissions, by allowing the indirect capitalization of surplus under the law permitting the reimbursement of the treasury for capital expenditures, have to that extent supported the actual cost basis.   Earning power was the test favored by Mr. Stevens of the Commission for the Second District and applied in two or three important decisions; but rate-making value has on several occasions been favored by the Commission for the First District.

This confusion of principles may or may not be justified.   Perhaps it can be shown that no one basis of capitalization is applicable in all cases.   But if that is true,—if it is really out of the question to fix a single definite standard,—the whole attempt to make capitalization correspond to assets is of doubtful value.   For the purpose of any such attempt is simply to give full publicity to the amount of the assets.

[1] Middlesex & Boston Rate Case, 2 Mass. P. S. C. 99 (1914), p. 111.
[2] R. L., ch. 112, pt. iii, sec. 145 (h).
[3] On this point see p. 95, *infra.*

If this purpose is to be attained, the basis for determining the amount must be well known to those who may rely on it. At present, the confusing variety of standards prevents any such knowledge. Only by referring to the reports of the public service commissions—and frequently not even then—can one tell what the nominal capitalization really means. But if anyone is willing to go to that trouble, he will find little use in par values; for he will be able to analyze directly the property accounts of the company without concerning himself about the nominal liabilities.

Practical Difficulties of Equalizing Capitalization and Investment

Even if public service commissions were ready to accept a definite basis of valuation for capitalization purposes, they would still face the almost impossible task of regulating securities on that basis. Indeed, one may say without exaggeration that only in exceptional cases have commissions been able to enforce an equality between capitalization and assets, no matter by what standards the assets may be measured. Two obstacles have prevented success: first, the difficulty of scaling down capitalization already excessive; second, the impossibility of marketing new securities always at par.

The first difficulty is due to the tardiness of the states in assuming control over public utility finance. Except in Massachusetts, security regulation was instituted only after years of almost unrestricted stock watering. The harm had already been done; it could not soon be undone. Drastic measures to enforce the reduction of excessive capitalization have been considered unwise as being not only unfair to present investors but also inexpedient because of the resulting injury to public utility credit pending the readjustment. Most public service commissions have therefore not insisted upon a scaling down of existing capitalization as a condition of the issuance of new securities. They have attempted simply to prevent further overissues in the future.[1]

This rule of letting existing securities alone has not been followed, however, in Massachusetts or in Texas. In both of these states the policy has been to require that existing capitalization shall not exceed the fair value of the property. Massachusetts has been able, usually though not always, to enforce this rule, since overcapitalization had never become very extensive there. Texas, on the other hand, has been much less successful. In 1893 it passed a law forbidding the issuance of bonds in excess of the " reasonable value " of the railway property; but it provided that, in exceptional cases, the face value of stocks and bonds combined might exceed the physical value of the property by not more than fifty per cent. Even with this modification the law discouraged new investments in Texas railways to such an extent that the legislature has been subsequently obliged to make it much less rigid. An act of 1901 provided that under certain conditions roads might issue securities to build extensions without regard to the capitalization of the existing property. Another act, in 1903, authorized the Railroad Commission to make similar allowance in the construction of double track and all necessary appurtenances. But even with these modifications, the Texas statute is still sharply criticized by railway officials as unduly restrictive.

Yet, with all the criticism that has been made of the Texas policy of scaling down existing capitalization, the law has not yet succeeded in making the outstanding securities correspond to the physical values. In 1916, according to the Texas Railroad Commission, the average value per

[1] See pp. 147-50, *infra.*

mile of line on those roads that had been appraised was $26,779, whereas the average amount of stocks and bonds on that same mileage was $31,174, leaving an excess of about 16 per cent over the assets.

From these experiences one is forced to conclude that the process of squeezing the water out of the present capitalization of railways will be a hopelessly slow one unless more radical measures are adopted by the federal government than have ever been attempted by our state governments. The only feasible means of equating capitalization and assets will be to require a complete reorganization of our railroad corporations. On many accounts, this may be the very best thing to do. It would fit in well with the plan for consolidation of railways into a few great systems and with the proposal to require federal incorporation of interstate carriers. In the final chapter of this treatise, we shall discuss the wisdom of some such plan. But whatever one may think of the proposal, one must admit that no less thoroughgoing measure—no more gradual scaling down of outstanding securities—is likely to bring about a correspondence between capitalization and assets during any period of time for which it is worth while to plan.

While the first practical difficulty which public service commissions have to face—the difficulty of scaling down existing capitalization—might thus be met by wholesale reorganization, not even this drastic device would solve the second problem—that of keeping new security issues equal to new investments. The difficulty is that stocks and bonds cannot regularly be sold at par. They cannot be sold at par for the reason that it is often necessary to issue securities of the same class. bearing the same rate of interest and dividends, at different times and under different conditions of the market. Even though the original issue were to be sold at its full face value, subsequent issues might not be saleable at half that price.

Public service commissions have tried in various ways to meet this difficulty.   In some states, commissions require companies that are unable to sell their stock for par to issue bonds or notes.   Even the bonds, to be sure, may have to be sold at a discount; but the discount may be amortized by charges against income.   This recourse to bonds as a means of avoiding the sale of stock below par cannot be too strongly condemned.   In the first place, so long as the bond discount remains unamortized, the purpose of preventing overcapitalization is not attained.   In the second place, the prevention of overcapitalization is not worth the cure of overbonding.   Most authorities agree that an excess of total par values is less serious than an overweight of debt.[1] Our public service laws, by stressing the former at the expense of the latter, are committing an error of the gravest character.

In other states, the commissions have frankly violated the orthodox principles of capitalization by permitting the sale of stock below par.[2]   A few of the eastern states have done this to a limited extent,[3] but in several western states, in California and Arizona, for example, the sale at a discount is the rule rather than the exception.

[1] See *Report of Railroad Securities Commission*, p. 25.

[2] Heilman, *op. cit.*, pp. 899-903; Barron, *Annals, Amer. Acad. Pol. & Soc. Science*, vol. lxxvi (March, 1918), pp. 185-7.

[3] For example, Maine requires that companies newly organized must sell their stocks at par, although old companies may be allowed to issue them at a discount. (See 1 Me. P. U. C. 51 [1915] and Applic. of Black Stream Elec. Co., P. U. R. 1915 C 361).   New York forbids by law the sale of stock below par; but the Public Service Commission for the 2d District has at least on one occasion sanctioned an evasion of this law by permitting the Erie Railroad to issue bonds at 85 which were convertible into stock at the rate of $200 in stock for every $100 in bonds (*Re* Erie R. R. Co., P. U. R. 1916 D 113).   The Wisconsin law prohibits the issuance of stock below par, but the Secretary of the Wisconsin Commission, Mr. H. L. Geisse, recently advocated a modification permitting sale at a discount (*Electric Railway Journal*, vol. xlvii [1916], pp. 602-3).

The fact that commissions have been obliged constantly to violate the accepted principle of equality between capitalization and assets is convincing evidence that the principle itself is unworkable. Indeed, so far as the writer can see, there is only one feasible way by which public service commissions might prevent capitalization from exceeding the investment; that is by keeping it ordinarily *far below* the investment. If railroads were as a general rule *undercapitalized*, they might never find it necessary to overstep the limit of fair value.

Precisely this method of procedure has been adopted in Massachusetts; and it is by means of this expedient that Massachusetts, alone of all the states, is able to claim that the capitalization of its public utilities (at least of its gas and electric companies) does not exceed their reasonable cost. For years this state has required public service corporations to sell their stocks at heavy premiums, whenever the market prices would justify those premiums. By this means, and by the consistent refusal of the regulating commissions to allow the capitalization of surplus, the market values of gas and electric stocks have for the most part been kept so high that the necessity of sale at a discount has been avoided.

This resort to undercapitalization as an alternative to overcapitalization has much to be said in its favor. Some persons, indeed, go so far as to hold that undercapitalization, so far from being an evil, is a positive good. To err on the safe side, they say, is an advantage. This view is very similar to the position taken by some accountants, that an undervaluation of assets for the property account should be encouraged.[1] But whatever one may think of the wisdom of undercapitalization with respect to industrial companies,

[1] This position, however, is not accepted by the best American authorities; see, for instance, H. R. Hatfield, *Modern Accounting* (New York, 1913), pp. 83-5.

one must admit that the practice, as applied to public service companies, has serious objections. The first and minor objection is that it would necessitate the sale of stock at premiums—that is, at prices above par. Now the experience of the stock market proves that investors are reluctant to pay high premiums for stocks. They feel that the par value indicates, to some extent, the normal value and that therefore a higher price is excessive. As a result, stock cannot be sold at a high premium unless the dividend rate is sufficient to yield a higher return on the investment than would have been necessary if the stock were selling around par. Of course, this higher yield is a tax on the rate-paying public.

Much more serious, however, is the second objection—that undercapitalization causes the public to underestimate the actual investment and therefore to exaggerate the rate of profits. Needless to say, such a misapprehension would be almost sure to do harm. It would probably lead to government action to reduce profits below a reasonable return—a result not only unfair to investors but also disastrous to railway credit. One of the most critical questions that will arise when the government establishes a really effective control over the profits of public service corporations is whether the public, when it knows the actual rate of profits in these enterprises, will be sufficiently liberal in its judgment of what constitutes a reasonable rate of return. There is danger that no adequate allowance will be made for the risks of the business. Some writers, indeed, aware of the popular tendency to begrudge more than a " savings-bank " rate of interest, have gone so far as to defend, or at least to condone, stock watering as a necessary safeguard against this prejudice. Of course, such a defense will not be accepted by anyone who really believes in democracy. The public has the right to know the facts even though it may

sometimes misuse those facts.   But it also follows that the
public should not be misled by an *understatement* of the
investment any more than by an *overstatement*.

Attempt to Equalize Capitalization and Assets Unnecessary

The conclusion to which the above discussion has led—
that the principle of correspondence between capitalization
and assets cannot be realized in practice—would be a gloomy
one were it not for the fact that it is as unnecessary as it
is impractical.   If the amount of the assets is known and
given full publicity, what need is there of attempting to set
up an equivalent face value in bonds and stocks?   The
balance sheets, if correctly kept, will show the actual investment.   All that is required is that the property accounts be
kept on a strict cost basis.

The trouble in the past has been that accurate records
have not been kept.   Companies have not only watered
their securities, but they have also concealed the presence
of that water by a corresponding overvaluation of the assets.
For this reason it has been quite impossible to find the actual
investment by consulting the balance sheets.   But this difficulty need not prevail in the future, for commissions are
requiring, with increasing strictness, that property accounts
should show the actual costs.

Only one serious objection can be urged against this
proposal to disregard par values.   So deeply set is the notion
that par values represent actual property, that people might
continue to attribute a significance to nominal capitalization
even after the true investment had been made public.   This
danger, as we saw in the previous chapter, is a real one.
But there is one possible way to overcome it—namely, to
issue capital stock without par value.   In the following
chapter, we shall discuss at length this much debated expedient.

SUMMARY

According to the generally accepted theory, nominal capitalization should correspond to the cost or to the value of the property. The standard for determining that cost or value has been much in dispute. No less than five possible bases have been given weight in the decisions of public service commissions. They are (1) rate-making value, (2) original investment, (3) actual cost including surplus derived from reinvested earnings, (4) market value, and (5) earning power.

The two bases that have been most generally favored by commissions are original investment and actual cost. Usually, one of these two has been used even when some other standard of value has been accepted for rate-making purposes. But the practice of commissions has been far from consistent; and no one basis has been adopted to the exclusion of all others.

No matter what basis the commissions have accepted as the test of proper capitalization, they have never been able to apply it rigorously in actual practice. The history of security regulation from its commencement in the nineties down to the present time testifies without exception in any state that the attempt to secure even an approximate balance between par values and actual investment is foredoomed to failure. It has resulted in the curbing of investment, as in Texas; in dangerous recourse to bonds because of inability to issue stock at par, as in New York; in the violation of the principle by undercapitalization, as in Massachusetts; or in the almost complete abandonment of the principle by overcapitalization, as in California and in other western states. Nowhere has it succeeded; nowhere can a public service commission point to the capitalization of companies under its jurisdiction as an indication of the actual investment in the property.

In view of these facts, the attempt to use nominal capitalization as a record of the investment should be frankly
abandoned.   In that case, either of two proposals might be
accepted: first, to allow the par values to remain but to
recognize them merely as a convenient fiction; second, to
issue capital stock without par, thus removing nominal capitalization as a source of deception.   Having noted a serious
objection to the first plan, we turn, in the following chapter,
to the alternative measure.

Social Sciences Sociales
University of Ottawa

CHAPTER IV

SHARES OF STOCK WITHOUT PAR VALUE [1]

[1] FAVORING THE REMOVAL OF PAR VALUES: *Proceedings of the New York Bar Association*, vol. xv (1892), p. 137 *et seq.*, and vol. xxxii (1909), pp. 270-82; Testimony of F. L. Stetson before the United States Industrial Commission, *Report*, vol. i (1900), p. 976; Edward M. Shepard, Annual Address before the Bar Association of New Hampshire, *Proceedings*, vol. ii, Old Series (1906), pp. 273-97; E. M. Shepard, "Corporate Capitalization and Public Morals," Address before the Illinois Bar Association, *Proceedings*, 1907, pt. ii, pp. 29-60; Frederick Dwight, "Par Value of Stock," *Yale Law Journal*, vol. xvi (1907), pp. 247-52; Chairman Frank W. Stevens, Decision *In re* N. Y. C. & H. R. R. and R. & E. Rapid Ry. Co., 1 P. S. C. R. (2d Dist. N. Y.) 294, 315 (1908); *Report of the Railroad Securities Commission* (1911), pp. 25-26; R. S. Lovett, *Statement before the Railroad Securities Commission, December 21, 1910* (New York, 1911?), pp. 16-18; R. S. Lovett, Testimony before the "Newlands Committee" (*Hearings before the Joint Committee on Interstate and Foreign Commerce Pursuant to Public J. Res. 25* . . . [Washington, 1916-18]), pp. 686, 707; Victor Morawetz, "Shares Without Nominal or Par Value," *Harvard Law Review*, vol. xxvi (1913), pp. 729-31; National Association of Railway Commissioners, *Proceedings*, 1913, pp. 197-98, and 1916, p. 241 *et seq.*; Frank White, *White on Corporations*, 8th ed. (New York, 1915), pp. 367-73; Hastings Lyon, *Corporation Finance* (Boston, 1916), pt. i, pp. 104-5.

OPPOSING THE REMOVAL: Arthur K. Kuhn, *A Comparative Study of the Law of Corporations* (New York, 1912), p. 115; William Z. Ripley, *Railroads: Finance and Organization* (New York, 1915), pp. 91-4; William Morse Cole, *Accounts, Their Construction and Interpretation*, rev. ed. (Boston, 1915), p. 207; Milton B. Ignatius, *The Financing of Public Service Corporations* (New York, 1918), pp. 78-83 (Doubts value of the removal as applied to public utilities subject to financial control by commission).

DESCRIPTIVE: John Adams, Jr., "Stocks and their Features—a Division and Classification," *Annals, Amer. Acad. Pol. and Soc. Science*, vol. xxxv (1910), pp. 526-7; Halford Erickson, *Regulation of Public Utilities:*

To those who accept the position, maintained in the previous chapter, that the attempt to secure equality between nominal capitalization and actual assets is neither feasible nor necessary, it will probably appear desirable to take the logical step of abandoning all pretense at such equality. Already the means of securing this object has been suggested, namely, the issuance of shares of stock without par values. But since this proposed measure has been criticized no less than favored, we shall devote a chapter to the discussion of its merits.

History of the Proposal [1]

Credit for originating this device for meeting the evils of watered stock is accorded to a committee of the New York Bar Association, which in 1892 proposed an amendment to the New York corporation laws by which private corporations should be permitted to issue shares of common stock without nominal value.[2] But the general principle of recognizing shares simply as participation certifi-

Three Discussions (Madison, Wis., 1911), pp. 61-2; Franklin Escher, "Without Par Value," *Harper's Weekly*, vol. lvi, May 11, 1912, p. 22; Thomas Mulvey, *Company Capitalization Control* (Ottawa, Ont., 1913), pp. xcvi-cv; Thomas Mulvey, "Blue Sky Law," *Canadian Law Times*, vol. xxxvi (1916), p. 43; Edward S. Mead, *Corporation Finance*, rev. ed. (New York, 1915), pp. 45-6; Charles W. Gerstenberg, *Materials of Corporation Finance*, 3d ed. (New York, 1915), pp. 43, 47; W. F. Moody, Jr., "The Value of Par Value," *Moody's Magazine*, vol. xix (1916), pp. 129-30; Albert W. Atwood, "New Devices of Finance," *McClure's Magazine*, vol. xlvii, July, 1916, pp. 64-5; Robert J. Bennett, *Corporation Accounting* (New York, 1917), pp. 89-91; Roy B. Kester, *Accounting: Theory and Practice*, vol. ii (New York, 1918), pp. 9-10, 20; F. H. Hurdman, "Capital Stock of No Par Value," *Journal of Accountancy*, vol. xxviii (1919), pp. 246-57; Arthur S. Dewing, *The Financial Policy of Corporations* (New York, 1920), pt. i, pp. 13-15.

[1] *Cf. White on Corporations*, 8th ed., pp. 371-73.

[2] New York Bar Association, *Proceedings*, vol. xv (January, 1892), p. 137.

cates was by no means new. The Bar Association committee referred to its use in German corporation finance, while a later writer noted that its " general adoption in practice . . . would bring us back to the joint-stock type of the Sixteenth, Seventeenth and Eighteenth centuries." [1]

A few years after this committee had made its original report, one of its members, Mr. F. L. Stetson, repeated the proposal in testifying before the United States Industrial Commission.[2] Again in 1909 the same committee, in a report to the Bar Association, renewed its recommendations [3] and submitted a draft bill for consideration by the New York Legislature.

In 1912, just twenty years after the first favorable report by the committee of the Bar Association, New York State took the lead by adopting the measure as a part of its corporation law. By this act business corporations are permitted to issue shares without par value, other than preferred shares with a preference as to principal.[4]

The example of New York was soon followed by other states. According to a recent count, nine others have already amended their corporation laws to permit the issuance of no-par shares: Maryland (1916), California (1917), Delaware (1917), Maine (1917), Virginia (1918), Illinois (1919), Pennsylvania (1919), New Hampshire (1919), and Ohio (1919).[5] It seems entirely probable

[1] Arthur K. Kuhn, *A Comparative Study of the Law of Corporations*, p. 115.

[2] *Report*, vol. i (1900), p. 976.

[3] *Proceedings*, vol. xxxii (Jan. 1909), pp 270-82.

[4] L. 1912, ch. 351, amended by L. 1917, ch. 500.

[5] F. H. Hurdman, "Capital Stock of No Par Value," *Journal of Accountancy*, vol. xxviii (1919), p. 255. Mr. Hurdman's timely article makes it unnecessary to present in this chapter an analysis of the provisions of the different statutes.

that within the next few years similar legislation will be generally adopted throughout the United States.

Up to the present time, however, most of the states that have provided for shares without par value have refused to extend the privilege to certain important classes of corporations. New York has set the example here by excepting from the provisions of the act not only banking companies but also public service corporations.[1] These latter companies were excluded because they are under the special supervision of the public service commissions; their securities can be issued only after being approved by the proper commission. Security regulation, it was believed, would prevent stock watering on the part of public utilities and would therefore make unnecessary the resort to no-par shares as a cure for overcapitalization. Whether or not such a belief is justified is a question that we shall discuss presently. But here we must note that the New York precedent of requiring the retention of par values for public utility securities has not been universally accepted. Even before the passage of the New York act, Mr. Stevens of the New York Public Service Commission for the Second District raised the question whether the removal of par values from public utility stocks would not be a wise action.[2] Two years later, in 1910, the Railroad Securities Commission gave its unqualified support to a proposal to permit interstate railways to issue shares of stock without par value.[3] Subsequently, members of the

---

[1] But the provision excluding public utilities has been circumvented, to some degree, by the holding company device. At least two public utility holding companies have issued common stock without par value under the New York law: the Interboro Consolidated Corporation and the Western Power Corporation. (See p. 105, note 3, *infra*.)

[2] *Re* N. Y. C. & H. R. R. and R. & E. Rapid Ry. Co., 1 P. S. C. R. (2nd Dist. N. Y.) 294, 315 (1908).

[3] *Report*, p. 25.

Wisconsin Railroad Commission[1] and of the California
Railroad Commission[2] have endorsed the proposal as applied to all public utilities.

Influenced, no doubt, by these favorable opinions, several
states have permitted public service corporations as well as
business corporations to issue shares without par value. The
recent amendments to the corporation laws of Delaware,
Maryland, Pennsylvania, and Virginia, providing for the
issue of stock without par value, contain no clause excluding public utilities from the provisions of the acts. In the
cases of Delaware[3] and Maryland,[4] however, there is some

---

[1] Mr. Roemer, Chairman of the Wisconsin Railroad Commission, in an
address before the Southern Gas Convention, Mobile, Ala., April 23,
1914, cited by Fred L. Holmes, *Regulation of Railroads and Public
Utilities in Wisconsin* (New York, 1915), p. 240. On the other hand,
Commissioner Erickson of the same commission expressed himself as
undecided as to the wisdom of permitting no-par shares: *Regulation of
Public Utilities: Three Discussions* (Madison, Wis., 1911), pp. 61-2.

[2] Commissioner Edgerton in decision *re* Pacific Gas & Elec. Co., P. U.
R. 1915 C 325, and the late Commissioner Eshleman in address before
the National Association of Railway Commissioners, *Proceedings of
Twenty Fifth Convention* (1913), pp. 197-98.

[3] In Delaware there is a law (Rev. Code 1915, ch. 65, sec. 102) which
requires that railroad companies incorporated and operating in that
state must indicate in their Articles of Association the amount of
capital stock, "which shall not be less than five thousand dollars for
every mile of road proposed to be constructed." A similar provision
applies to electric railways, except that the amount is here two thousand
instead of five thousand. I am informed by the Secretary of State of
Delaware that his office regards this law as preventing the issuance of
stock of no par value by companies of the above-mentioned class. He
writes: "If you should have no capital stock [with a par value] of a
corporation incorporated under the provisions of section 102 of the
General Corporation Laws, there would be no way whereby this office
could know that the fourth paragraph of this section would be com-
plied with."

[4] In Maryland the right of railroad corporations to issue shares without par value is made doubtful by a provision of the Maryland statutes
(Annotated Code, Article 23, sec. 264) stating that the capital stock of

doubt whether railroad corporations may issue no-par shares in view of the fact that the older statutes applying specifically to that class of corporations may perhaps be held to require the use of stock having a par value. The law of California specifically provides that all public service corporations may issue stock without par, but only with the approval of the Railroad Commission. Illinois and New Hampshire exclude railroads but do not exclude other public utilities. Ohio and Maine follow the New York precedent by excepting all public service corporations.

During the first few years after the passage of the New York act of 1912, only a few corporations took advantage of the privilege of issuing stock without nominal value. There was a natural hesitation lest the new device might not prove popular with the investing public. But experience soon proved such fears to be groundless; investors have accepted no-par shares quite as readily as any others.

Judging from the newspaper prospectuses of recent months, one may conclude that the use of common shares without par value has now become the rule rather than the exception for newly incorporated companies.[1] Even several of the large older corporations have exchanged their former shares for the newer type.[2] Only a few public service companies, however, have as yet followed the example of the industrials.[3] This is doubtless to be explained by

a railroad corporation shall be divided into shares of fifty dollars each. I am informed by Mr. James Piper of the Baltimore law firm of Piper, Yellot, Hall & Carey that the courts have not yet rendered a decision as to whether or not this clause applying to railways is superseded by the subsequent act permitting corporations in general to issue no-par shares.

[1] *E. g.*, Cuba Cane Sugar Corp., Kennecott Copper Corp., Submarine Boat Corp., Allied Packers, Inc., United Retail Stores Corp. (preferred stock also without par), Atlantic Lobos Oil Co., Shaffer Oil & Refining Co.

[2] *E. g.*, B. F. Goodrich Co. and General Motors Corp.

[3] *E. g.*, Penn Central Light & Power Co., incorporated in Pennsyl-

the fact that it was not until the year 1916 that any state permitted such action on the part of utility corporations and that, since then, the financing of public service enterprises has been at a very low ebb.

Advantages

The main object of the reform that we have been discussing is to remove the fictitious element in corporation finance. The par value of a share of stock can have no significance except in so far as it represents actual assets. In the theory of the law, that is just what it is supposed to represent; in practice, it represents nothing of the kind. This divergence between theory and practice is due in part to the lax corporation laws of several states; but it is also due to another cause which cannot be removed; namely, to the impossibility of issuing stock always at par regardless of the conditions of the market.

Since, therefore, par value cannot serve its intended purpose of indicating the actual capital, it may better be removed instead of being allowed to remain as a source of

vania (common and preference shares without par value). At least two public utility holding companies, incorporated in New York, have issued common shares without par value: the Western Power Corp. (of California) and the Interboro Consolidated Corp., a company holding the securities of the New York City railway companies (see p. 103, note 1, *supra*). A number of voluntary associations, organized under the Massachusetts law to hold the securities of public utility companies, have issued participation shares without par value: *e. g.*, Boston & Worcester Electric Companies, Boston Suburban Electric Companies, and Central Massachusetts Light and Power Co. In the first two cases, both the preferred and the common shares are without par value, while in the last, the preferred shares retain the par value. The Chicago Elevated Railways, a voluntary association organized under the laws of Massachusetts, has issued preferred and common shares which are "expressed as of a par value of $100," but which are carried on the books at no valuation (see p. 119, note 1, *infra*). The Chicago Railways Co., an Illinois corporation, has issued capital stock of the merely nominal amount of $100,000; this stock is held in trust, and against it are issued 265,100 "participation certificates" without par value.

deceit to unwary investors. The removal may be expected
to have the wholesome effect of forcing the attention of
investors upon the value of the property behind their securities rather than on the nominal amount of those securities.
This result, if it can be achieved, will mark a great advance
in corporation finance; for too often have investors been
deceived by their assumption that a large nominal capitalization means an equally large investment. To eliminate
this danger of deception would be to remove one of the
serious evils of stock watering.

To be sure, it must be admitted that the mere use of
shares without par value will not *alone* cure the evils of
stock watering; for the removal of par value does not remove *all* the sources of deception to which the unwary investor is subject. On this point a word of caution has
already been uttered; [1] and it will be repeated in a later
section of the present chapter in order to emphasize the
need for further safeguards. But the truth of this admission does not weaken the force of the fact that *one* source
of deception may be removed; and that consideration alone
justifies the reform.

The opinion has sometimes been advanced that the use
of shares without par value, while suitable for business corporations, should not be extended to railroads or to other
public service corporations whose securities are subject to
control by a government commission. This view accounts
for the failure of New York and other states to include
public utilities among those corporations that may issue
stock of no par value. Regulation of securities is thought
to be an alternative to the removal of par value; the one
measure aims to prevent stock watering by making the par
value equal the investment, while the other would secure
the same end by abolishing the par value entirely. [2]

[1] P. 57, *supra.*

[2] *Cf.* Ignatius, *Financing of Public Service Corporations* (1918), p. 83,

If commission regulation could in fact secure an approximate balance between nominal capitalization and actual investment, one might concede the wisdom of retaining the par value of public utility stocks. But, as we have already noted in the previous chapter, no such results have been secured, nor is there any likelihood of success in the future. In a large number of cases, par values will either understate or exaggerate the actual contribution made by the investors. Therefore as long as par values are retained, they will remain a source of misinformation.

Of course, one may freely admit that careful control of securities by a commission will greatly reduce the danger of deceit occasioned by fictitious par values. Not only will the more extreme forms of stock inflation be prevented, but, what is even more important, the investing public will be informed as to the actual capital in the enterprise, so that it may discount any excessive stock issues. Yet, with all these cautions, the danger of misunderstanding is merely minimized but not removed so long as the par value remains. The " magic of par value " is too potent to be entirely eliminated by a program of publicity.[1]

But there is even a stronger reason for removing the par value of public utility stocks. Unless it is removed, commissions will still feel under obligation to *strive* for an approximate equality between capitalization and investment. Of course they will not succeed,—they never have succeeded, —but instead of abandoning all effort to secure an equality, they will make the attempt to come as near to a balance as is at all practicable. They will permit the issue of stock below par—but only as a last resort, rather than as a regular and proper procedure. This, at least, has been the tendency of state commissions up to the present time; and it is almost sure to continue to be the policy in the future, owing to the popular hostility to stock watering.

[1] See pp. 59-61, *supra*.

This half-way measure—this *partial* abandonment of the attempt to make capitalization correspond to assets—is in many ways more dangerous than would be the complete recognition of par values as a mere fiction. In the first place, it serves to strengthen rather than to weaken the illusion on the part of investors that par value represents the actual investment. In the second place, it causes commissions to approve the resort to excessive bond issues as a means of avoiding the necessity of selling stock below par. This second tendency was noted in the last chapter as a serious objection to security regulation as now practised by state commissions; but it is almost inevitable as long as commissions are under pressure to prevent the sale of stock at a discount. The only adequate means of removing this pressure is to remove the par value, so that stock may be issued at whatever prices are justified by market conditions.

One special advantage of shares without par value deserves particular emphasis at the present time; namely, their convenience in cases of reorganization and consolidation. Few will deny that any program of railway reform has little chance of solving the present difficulties of our interstate transportation systems that does not involve, first, a reorganization of unwieldy financial structures and, second, a consolidation of certain independent roads into larger groups. Heretofore, however, both of these financial operations have usually resulted in an increase rather than a decrease of nominal liabilities. It is true that, in recent years, when reorganizations and consolidations have been subject to the approval of state public service commissions, the tendency to inflation has been partly eliminated. But even in these cases, commissions have usually found it impossible to enforce a rigid scaling-down of capitalization to the point of equality with the assets. The obstacle has been the reluctance of security holders to accept new securities of a lower *par value* than that of the stocks and bonds which they are asked to surrender. To be sure, the commissions might have insisted on such an exchange; but in the case of consolidations, that requirement might have caused the stockholders to abandon their plan for a merger, while in the case of reorganizations, it would have led the security holders to decline either to pay assessments or to subscribe for new securities.

The use of shares without par value, however, will make it much easier to consolidate or to reorganize on a sound financial basis. Because of the removal of par values, there will not be the same need for a stringent reduction in the number of shares; the holders of one share of old stock may be given with less reluctance one share of new stock, since the new stock indicates nothing as to the amount of investment represented by each share.

The special convenience of shares without par value in the above cases was noted by the Railroad Securities Commission. Its statement on this point is worth quoting in full:

Where two roads have consolidated whose shares have different market values, it has been the custom to equalize the difference by the issue of extra shares of the consolidated company to the owners of the higher priced stock. This practice has always tended to produce increase of capital issues, and may readily cause the new stock to be issued for a consideration less than its par value. The only alternative was to scale down some of the old stocks; and this often involved serious difficulties, both of business policy and of law. By the simple expedient of omitting the dollar mark from the new shares, the number can be adjusted to the demands of financial convenience, without danger of misrepresentation or suspicion of unfairness to anyone.[1]

In the case of reorganizations, the advantage of shares with-

[1] At this point the opinion of the Securities Commission seems over-optimistic. Even when the par value is removed, there is some danger

out par value is even more obvious. It is here that the necessity and justice of getting money from stockholders is greatest. It is here that the impossibility of getting them to pay par for new shares is most conspicuous. We believe that in such cases the public interest would be subserved and the speedy rehabilitation of the roads promoted, by requiring the conversion of the common stock and encouraging the conversion of the preferred stock into shares without par value; the certificates simply indicating the proportionate or preferential claims of the holders upon assets and upon such profit as might from time to time be earned.[1]

Alleged Objections

Having noted the advantages to be gained by authorizing railroads to issue shares without par value, we must now discuss the supposed objections. At least six criticisms have been made, each of which we shall consider in turn.

1. *That the removal of par value will encourage inflation by making easy the issue of an excessive number of shares.* This point was discussed by the Railroad Securities Commission. It remarked:

The danger of inflation deserves more serious consideration. We believe, however, that it is more apparent than real, because shareholders will be jealous of permitting other shareholders to acquire shares in the association except at full market value, and will not permit the issue of such shares to themselves at prices so low as seriously to impair the market or other value of their holdings. Shares either with or without par value, and whether sold at par or above par or be-

---

that an increased number of shares may give a false impression of an increase in value. On this point see pp. 126-27, *infra*. However, it can hardly be doubted that the use of no-par shares will *reduce*, even though it does not *remove*, the danger.

[1] *Report*, p. 26.

low it, should, except in cases of consolidation and reorganization, be offered in the first instance to existing shareholders pro rata.[1]

But the above comments of the Securities Commission leave some important points unanswered. In the first place, it is not clear what is meant by inflation in the case of no-par stock. If each share represents, not a fixed amount, but merely a fractional interest in the total capital, whatever that capital may be, is any significance to be placed on the number of shares into which the total stock is divided? And if the number of shares does indeed have a significance,—if the possibility of inflation still exists after the par value is removed,—is the Securities Commission correct in assuming that the self-interest of the shareholders will prevent such inflation? An answer to the first question has already been suggested in an earlier chapter.[2] There we saw that the danger of inflation persists in spite of the removal of par value. Further discussion of this point is deferred to a later section of the present chapter. As to the second question, it must be admitted that the reply of the Securities Commission is not entirely convincing. In the past, when stock had a par value, the self-interest of shareholders did not suffice to prevent inflation. Why, then, should it suffice with the par value removed?

One must concede, then, that the danger of inflation remains in spite of the use of no-par shares. Indeed, one might argue that, in the absence of all restrictions on the issuance price, the danger may even be increased. That fact, however, does not condemn the removal of par value from the shares of public utilities and railroads. For, since

[1] *Report*, p. 26.
[2] P. 57, *supra*.

the issue of shares is to be subject to control by commission, the danger of inflation is equally well guarded against, whether the par value is removed or not.

2. *That the removal of par value will encourage the flotation of shares of low market value—a result conducive to overspeculation.* This point is somewhat similar to the previous one. Ripley gives it as one reason for his opposition to the use of no-par stock. " The abolition of par value," he says, " permitting carriers to issue capital stock for relatively small sums in cash, cannot but encourage speculative interest in railways—an element of danger much to be deplored." [1]

This view accepts a prevalent assumption that a low market value gives shares a speculative character. But to what extent is this assumption justified? To be sure, it must be admitted that, in the experience of the stock-market, low-priced shares have generally been of a speculative nature. But the relation is not to any considerable extent one of cause and effect. What gives these shares their speculative character is the low value, not so much of each separate share, but of the total stock issue as compared with the value of the entire property represented by both bonds and stocks. In other words, it is primarily the narrow equity of the stock issue as a whole which makes the shares subject to such wide market fluctuations. The extreme width of the fluctuations is due, first, to the fact that a *slight* change in the earning power of the property will cause a *great* change in the balance of the earnings available for the stock, and, second, to the fact that a controlling interest in the enterprise may be bought with a relatively small outlay of capital. Both of theses factors tend to make the stock a gamble rather than an investment.

[1] *Railroads: Finance and Organization* (New York, 1915), p 94.

The fact that low market values *per share* have been a symptom rather than a cause of speculation is well exemplified in the case of the Rock Island financial manœuvres, so well described by Ripley.[1] It was the narrowing of the controlling interest to an investment of only about fifty million dollars and the complete wiping out of the equity of the holding company's stocks which made the securities a football for speculation. Would anyone anticipate similar results if Pennsylvania capital stock, or Northwestern preferred or common were to be divided into one-dollar shares, leaving the total investment unchanged? Does anyone suppose that Liberty bonds are much more speculative because they are issued in fifty-dollar denominations instead of merely in thousand-dollar denominations—or, on the other hand, that mining stocks would become steady investments if they were only marketed in hundred-dollar shares instead of in one-dollar shares?

One must admit that there is a *certain minimum* of truth in the assumption that the low price of a share tends in itself to make it speculative. It arises from the fact that people of small means can afford to speculate more freely in low-priced stock. But if public policy requires the curbing of this small-scale gambling, much more effective means may be found than the retention of a par value. For example, a minimum tax might be placed on the transfer of all shares of stock in whatever amounts, so that the small transaction would be discouraged by the disproportionately high tax. Or, again, the law might fix a minimum price below which shares without par value might not be issued. Indeed, that very thing is done by New York State, which requires that shares without par value must represent a capital of at least five dollars or some multiple thereof per share. Instead of five dollars, the minimum might be set

[1] *Op. cit.*, pp. 524-32.

at fifty or one hundred dollars, or at any other desired amount.

3. *That the removal of par value will release stockholders from their liability to creditors for the full payment of their subscriptions.* Under the limited-liability laws, stockholders in corporations are liable for the corporate debts only to the amount of their stock subscription as measured by the par value of the shareholdings. If a creditor finds that stock has been issued without a corresponding payment to the company in cash or property, he may sue the stockholders for unpaid claims up to the amount still due on the stock subscription. Now, some writers fear that the abolition of par value will take from creditors this safeguard. For in that case there can be no liability to make good the difference between the nominal value of the stock and the amount actually paid in on that stock.[1]

This objection, however, can readily be met. The recent state laws permitting the issuance of shares without par value have met it in two ways. The first way, adopted by New York, California, and Maine, is to forbid the issuance of part-paid shares and to make the corporate directors personally liable for violation of this provision.[2] The second way, adopted by Delaware, is to permit the issuance of part-paid shares, but to make shareholders liable to the

---

[1] Ripley makes this criticism (*Railroads: Finance and Organization,* p. 94).

[2] For instance, the Maine law (L. 1917, ch. 144) reads: " No corporation formed pursuant to section one hundred and fifteen hereof shall begin to carry on business or shall incur any debts until the amount of capital stated in its certificate of incorporation shall have been fully paid in money or in property taken at its actual value. In case the amount of capital stated in its certificate of incorporation shall be increased as hereinafter provided, such corporation shall not increase the amount of its indebtedness then existing until it shall have received in money or property the amount of such increase of its stated capital."

corporation's creditors for all amounts due on their sub-scriptions.[1] This second expedient retains the same safe-guards that are present under the old system, with a simple modification to the effect that stockholders are liable *for whatever amount they have agreed to pay* rather than for an amount equal to the par value of their shares. So far from taking away any protection from creditors, this new measure may even increase the protection. Up to the present time, as every student of corporation finance knows, the laws making shareholders liable for full pay-ment on their stock have proved but a very meager safe-guard to creditors. A part of the difficulty has been due to the unwillingness of courts to hold shareholders responsible for full payment in cases where it was impossible for the issuing company to market its stock at par.[2] But where the liability is fixed, not by a par value, but by the amount subscribed for each particular issue, the reasonableness of the liability for any unpaid balance is so clear that a much more rigid enforcement of the law may be expected.

4. *That the removal of par value will make it easier for promoters to retain an excessive amount of the stock as a reward for their services.* In the past, one of the great evils connected with the promotion of American railroad corporations has been the exorbitant profits that promoters have made by taking an excessive amount of stock in pay-ment for their activities. Of course, the disproportionate interest that the promoter secures lessens by so much the

[1] The Delaware Law (L. 1917, ch. 113, sec. 10) reads. " . . . in the case of stock without par value, this liability [for the unpaid balance on subscriptions to stock] shall be limited to the unpaid balance of the consideration for which such stock was issued by the corporation, which said sum or proportion thereof may be recovered as provided for in section 49 of this Chapter . . . "

[2] *Cf.* Handley *v.* Stutz, 139 U. S. 417 (1891).

value of the holdings of *bona fide* investors; it exacts a tribute which must be paid either by the other stockholders in the form of lower dividends or by the public in the form of higher transportation rates. It is feared by some that this evil, bad enough under the old order of things, may become even more serious if the par value is removed from the stock. The dollar sign, it is thought, does serve to some extent to restrain the promoter from taking an excessive amount of stock. It serves to impress upon the other shareholders the size of the slice which the promoter proposes to cut for himself. " Ten thousand shares " of stock as a reward to the promoter might not sound as exorbitant as a " million dollars of stock ". [1]

The force of this objection, however, may be seriously doubted. Indeed, it is at least open to argument that the removal of par value will decrease rather than increase the difficulty referred to. As long as par values remain, it is possible for promoters, simply by inflating the nominal capitalization, to conceal the fact that they have cut away a large slice of the stock. Investors are given one hundred dollars or more of stock for every hundred dollars that they contribute; they are quite unaware that they are paying partly for genuine stock and partly for water. Suppose, now, that the par values are removed. Is there not some reason to suppose that investors will be more rather than less critical of the disposition of the stock by promoters, now that the deceptive nominal values are not pres-

---

[1] This point has been called to my attention by a friendly critic, who writes as follows: " The dollar sign does afford some small protection to the investor as against the promoter who allots a disproportionate amount of shares to himself, or to others, for services rendered. It makes comparisons easier. If I pay $100,000 for a thousand shares, the issuing of another thousand in exchange for property worth only $50,000 is a rather more obvious discrimination than if I pay $100,000 for, say, a one-thousandth interest in a company which gives a similar fractional interest for property of whatever value."

ent? At least, it seems reasonably clear that promoters will not find it easier to withdraw excessive profits when the par value is eliminated than when the par value was retained.

5. *That par values are necessary, or at least desirable, as a convenient device for accounting.* This view has been expressed by several authorities in accounting. William Morse Cole, for example, objects to the removal of par values on the ground that " it neglects a point most important for the accountant—namely, that some sort of capitalization is necessary for any scientific bookkeeping." [1] Unfortunately, Cole does not state the grounds for this opinion. Ripley, who takes a similar view, is more specific. After noting other objections to the use of stock without par value, he writes :

And what is of great importance for the future under the growing tendency to ascertain the physical valuation of the property, all standards by which to readily measure the reasonableness of the general scale of charges disappear. The scientific accountant must have some absolute basis for his bookkeeping. Without some such starting point the relation between a fair return upon the investment and a surplus arising either from issue of shares at a premium or inordinately high rates becomes difficult to state. [2]

Ripley's argument seems to be that without par value it is difficult to set up accurate accounts on the liabilities side of the balance sheet and to distinguish clearly between share capital on the one hand and surplus on the other. As a matter of fact, however, is not the situation quite the contrary? The distinction between capital and surplus is

[1] *Accounts, Their Construction and Interpretation*, rev. and enl. ed. (Boston, 1915), p. 207.
[2] *Railroads: Finance and Organization*, p. 94.

even more clearly and simply shown without the fiction of par values. In that case, the proper accounting procedure is simply this: Stock is credited to the Capital Stock Account, not at its face value, but at the price for which it has actually been sold.[1] Where the shares have a par value, a different rule of accounting applies. Here, stock is credited to the Capital Stock Account at par, regardless of the issuing price; any excess or deficit in the actual proceeds is carried to a Premium and Discount Account. Under the former procedure, the total contribution by stockholders is shown in a single account; under the latter, it can be arrived at only by a process of addition or subtraction.

The above points may be made clearer by an example. Suppose that a company has issued one thousand shares of stock at $150 per share and suppose that the company has a surplus from reinvested earnings of $50,000. Now if the stock has a par value of $100 per share, the facts will be shown by the following entries in the accounts:

Assets		*Liabilities*	
Property	$200,000	Capital Stock	$100,000
		Stock Premium	50,000
		Surplus from Earnings	50,000
	$200,000		$200,000

[1] Although the above accounting procedure seems to have been adopted by most corporations that have issued shares of stock without par value, it has not been universally adopted. For example, the Kennecott Copper Corporation enters its capital stock on the books at a valuation of five dollars per share in spite of the fact that much of its stock was issued at a price of fifty dollars per share. The reason for this retention by the Kennecott Corporation of a nominal value for bookkeeping purposes is doubtless to be found in the peculiar provisions of the New York corporation law, discussed below, pp. 121-24. Still another method of accounting has been adopted by the Chicago Elevated Railways, a voluntary association. This company carries its participation shares (preferred and common) on the balance sheet at no valuation. It then sets up a single proprietorship account.

If, on the other hand, the stock is without par value, then the *same* facts will be shown on the balance sheet as follows:

Assets		Liabilities	
Property	$200,000	Capital Stock	$150,000
		Surplus	50,000
	$200,000		$200,000

The second statement makes even more clear than the first the distinction between the original investment (Capital Stock) and the surplus. It does this by eliminating the stock premium (or discount) account. The removal of this account, so far from being a loss, is a great gain. Of what possible use is it to enter into a separate account an amount by which the proceeds of stock exceed or fall short of a fixed nominal sum (the par value)? Moreover, the presence of a stock premium has sometimes led to the payment of unearned dividends, because the premium has been treated like income from earnings, to be paid out in dividends instead of being kept intact as part of the corporate capital.[1]

We conclude, then, that accounting has much to gain and little to lose by the removal of a necessarily fictitious par value.

[1] *Cf.* Mead, *Corporation Finance* (1915), p. 206. It is true that some authorities have defended the practice of paying out premiums in dividends. Ignatius seems to think that this may be proper. He says: ". . if the reason for the collection of premiums is that of equalizing the interests of the new stockholders with those of the old, should not the additional payment by the new stockholders be carried to the same account which registers the value-over-par interest of the old, to wit, the Corporate Surplus or Deficit account?" (*Financing of Public Service Corporations*, p. 75). But the objection to that practice is that shareholders may be deceived as to the actual earnings of the company; they may fail to see that the proceeds from premiums are an extraordinary source of profit and therefore not to be counted upon as a regular annual source of income. Receipts from premiums and receipts from earnings should therefore be kept quite distinct—the former being treated as an increase in *capital* and the other as *income*.

6. *That the removal of par value will open the way to
the impairment of capital.* One of the evils against which
corporation laws have attempted to guard is the impairment
of capital by the payment of unearned dividends. Where
the amount of capital is presumed to be determined by the
par value of the stock, the law forbids the disbursement of
this capital in the form of dividends. If, now, the par
value is to be removed, it is thought that the distinction between capital and divisible surplus may be harder to
maintain—that unscrupulous directors may be able to en-
croach upon the capital without fear of legal redress.

But if the new laws permitting the issue of shares without par value are drawn so as to make clear the distinction
between capital and surplus, and if they provide a definite
penalty against encroachment on capital, there is no reason
to anticipate any more difficulty with the new kind of stock
than with the old. Indeed, as has already been pointed
out, the distinction between capital and surplus is even
more easy to maintain when the par value is removed than
when it is retained. All proceeds from the sale of stock
are to be considered capital; all reinvested earnings are to
be credited to surplus.

It must be admitted, however, that some of the present
laws permitting the issuance of shares without par value
are very defective at just this point. The New York statute, for instance, may be criticized here. According to this
law, any corporation, in order to issue common stock without par value, must state in its certificate of incorporation
the amount of capital with which the corporation will carry
on business, which amount shall be not less than the amount
of the preferred stock (if any) authorized to be issued
with a preference as to principal, and in addition thereto a
sum equivalent to five dollars or to some multiple of five
dollars for every share authorized to be issued, other than

preferred stock; but in no event shall the amount of such capital be less than five hundred dollars.[1]

The law further provides that

No such corporation shall declare any dividend which shall reduce the amount of its capital below the amount stated in the certificate as the amount of capital with which the corporation will carry on business.[2]

Now let us note the implications of these provisions. Instead of defining the capital of the corporation as the *entire amount* of the proceeds realized by the sale of stock, and instead of requiring that no part of these proceeds may be paid out in dividends, the law simply states a "minimum capital" of five dollars (or some multiple) per share of common stock, which must be on hand before the commencement of business, and which may not be disbursed in dividends. But suppose that a corporation states its minimum capital at five dollars per share in its certificate of incorporation, and then issues its stock at fifty dollars per share.[3] Does the law regard that extra forty-five dollars per share as capital? And would the law prevent the distribution of those forty-five dollars per share as a cash dividend? Apparently not.

If this interpretation of the law is correct, it indicates a very serious defect. For the corporation is then free to treat a large part of the proceeds from the sale of stock either as surplus or as capital, whichever it desires. It is hardly necessary to point out the dangers of such a situation. Creditors who have relied on a fifty-dollar equity

[1] L. 1912, ch. 351, sec. 19.

[2] *Ibid.*, sec. 20.

[3] That is precisely the case with the Kennecott Copper Corporation, which carries its common shares at a valuation of five dollars per share although a considerable portion of the stock was issued on the basis of fifty dollars per share. See p. 119, note 1, *supra.*

behind every share of common stock may awaken to the fact that all but five dollars per share has been distributed among stockholders; shareholders may suddenly learn that they have been receiving dividends, not out of income, but out of the very capital that they contributed.

So great is the danger from this defective law, that if it could not be removed, it would be enough to condemn the entire plan of issuing shares without par value. But as a matter of fact the trouble can easily be remedied. The defect of the New York law is that *it does not go far enough* in removing par values; it still retains par value to the extent that it fixes the stated capital at a certain amount per share. It is a compromise between the old principle and the new; and like so many compromises, it is worse than either of the two extremes.

Unfortunately, several other states have followed the example of New York in providing that the minimum capital which must not be impaired by dividends is to be a certain fixed sum per share. The laws of Maine and Ohio are in this respect almost identical with that of New York, while California has adopted a similar provision with respect to business corporations although not with respect to public utilities. In other states, however, a different principle prevails: the *entire proceeds* of the sale of stock are counted as constituting the capital. The laws of Pennsylvania[1] and Maryland[2] seem specifically to indicate this;

[1] L. 1919, no. 363, sec. 3: " For the purposes of this act, the 'stated capital' of a corporation issuing shares without nominal or par value shall be the capital with which the corporation will begin business, as stated in the certificate of incorporation or reorganization . . . plus any net additions thereto, or minus any net deductions therefrom: Provided, That 'stated capital' shall not include any net profits or surplus earnings so long and during such period as the same may be paid out in the form of dividends under the provisions of section eight of this act . . . "

Ibid., sec. 8: " No corporation having shares without nominal or par

while in Delaware, Illinois,[1] and Virginia one is left to infer the same in the absence of provisions to the contrary.

Limitations of the Measure as a Remedy for the Evils of Stock Watering

Although most of the objections urged against the use of shares without par value are unwarranted, many of the claims in its favor are equally unfounded. Frequently it has been advocated as in itself offering a cure for the evil of overcapitalization. Business men have favored it, not as a mere aid to the government in its control over public utility securities, but as an all-sufficient substitute for such control. Judge Lovett, for instance, in a statement before the Railroad Securities Commission, held that

the issuance of shares, as shares, without attributing to them a value, which of necessity varies and is more or less misleading, rationally solves all the problems about ' watered ' stock,

value, issued under the provisions of this act, shall declare or pay any dividend out of capital or out of anything except net profits or surplus earnings."

[2] L. 1916, ch. 596, sec. 9: " For the purpose of any rule of law or of any statutory provision (except as in this section otherwise provided) relating to the amount of such stock issued, the amount of such stock issued shall be taken to be the amount of cash or the value of the services or property (determined by the board of directors as required by law) for which such stock has been issued."

[1] The Illinois law, to be sure, requires that a company, in order to carry on business, must have a capital equal to at least five dollars per share of stock of no par value. There seems to be nothing in the law, however, to indicate that this five dollars is anything but the *minimum* —nothing, that is, to indicate that if a corporation issued its shares for more than five dollars per share, it would be permitted to pay out in dividends all except five dollars per share. To that extent, I take it, it differs from the New York law, which, by forbidding a corporation to pay any dividends that would reduce the capital *below* the minimum stated in its certificate of incorporation, would seem by implication to permit the disbursement in dividends of any sums received from the sale of stock *in excess* of the minimum five dollars.

and dispenses absolutely with the necessity for any legislation upon that subject.[1]

Similar views were expressed by the Committee of the New York Bar Association.[2] Even Commissioner Erickson of Wisconsin seemed to think that this position might possibly be tenable.[3]

Other writers, however, have strongly denied this contention. Kuhn, who refers to the use of shares without face value in the 16th to 18th centuries, says:

Historical experience teaches that the aliquot shares attained values as fictitious as those often found at the present time, producing all of the evils attending overcapitalization.[4]

He therefore concludes that abolition of par value will accomplish no good and will do away with a convenient mathematical device. Ignatius, while not denying that the removal of par values may be useful in the case of private business corporations, warns against expecting too much from it. He says:

Removing the par value is not enough; standing by itself that change does not interpose any obstacle to the practices which have been the means of working overcapitalization heretofore. Take, for instance, the device of issuing shares in exchange for property or service accepted at an overvaluation; if the shares have a par value, the acceptor of the shares may reap a profit by reselling to those who will assume that the actual price paid for them upon issue equaled that paid for other shares of the same issue. If on the other hand the shares have no par value, the acceptor of the shares in exchange for property or services has precisely the same opportunity for

---

[1] *Statement before the Railroad Securities Commission, op. cit.,* p. 17.

[2] *Proceedings,* vol. xv (1892), p. 138.

[3] *Regulation of Public Utilities: Three Discussions,* p. 62.

[4] *A Comparative Study of the Law of Corporations,* p. 115.

profit by reselling to those who will likewise assume that those shares had been issued for consideration equaling that paid for other shares of that issue, since all shares of the one issue are required to be offered for sale upon like consideration.[1]

It is not necessary to accept Kuhn's view of the uselessness of the proposal, or to admit Ignatius's doubt as to its advisability under commission regulation of securities, to see a large measure of truth in these remarks. After all, the abandonment of par value merely gets rid of one of the deceptive figures in corporation accounting. It does not substitute the correct data. A share, it indicates, is simply a fraction of a given total investment. But how large is this total investment? That remains to be shown. Nothing less than government supervision can insure a correct statement of the actual investment.

It cannot be too strongly emphasized that the use of shares without par value will not of itself remove the danger of stock inflation. This point has been already discussed in an earlier chapter.[2] How is it possible, one asks, to inflate shares without par value, when each share is now supposed to represent, not a definite amount of investment, but merely a certain *fractional interest* in the total property? The answer is that shares, even shares of no par value, will not be regarded by investors as representing mere fractional claims. People do not think in those terms. They think of a share as representing *an amount* not *a fraction*. That amount is determined in their minds largely by the market quotations and by the established dividend. If, then, the number of shares is doubled without any increase in earning power,—say, by the issue of a stock dividend of one hundred per cent,—investors will probably fail to see that each share now repre-

[1] *Financing of Public Service Corporations* (1918), pp. 81-82.
[2] P. 57, *supra*.

sents an earning power of only half its former amount.
The market values of the new shares will therefore be inflated. By taking advantage of this failure of investors to
discount the increase, unscrupulous financiers will be able
to profit in the future, as they have profited in the past, by
issuing shares in excessive amounts.

We conclude, then, that only when accompanied by more
positive forms of regulation does the device of shares
without par value promise much relief from the evils of
overcapitalization. Its rôle is the modest though significant
one of removing a fictitious statement in order to leave a
clean sheet for the correct information. The more am-
bitious part claimed for it of solving in itself the problem
of stock watering, it is wholly unfitted to play.

Proper Scope of Application—Should it include Preferred Stock?

If we accept the general principle of the proposal to issue
shares without nominal value, two questions arise as to the
proper extent of its application in railroad law.   First,
should it apply to preferred stocks as well as to common?
Second, should it be compulsory or simply optional?

On the first point the present laws differ.   Delaware,
Ohio, and Virginia exclude all preferred stock from the
provisions of their acts; New York and Maine exclude preferred stock with a preference as to principal; Maryland
excludes stock preferred as to dividends and subject to re-
demption as well as stock preferred as to principal.   Illinois, Pennsylvania and New Hampshire, on the other hand,
make no restrictions as to the class of stock which may be
issued without par value. California, in its law applying to
industrial companies, follows the New York precedent by
excluding stock preferred as to principal, but in the similar
statute applying to public utilities, it provides that a com-

pany not only may but *must* issue all classes of stock without par value provided it issues any class without par.

At least two reasons may be given for retaining the par value on preferred shares, even when it is removed from the common. *First,* this distinction between the two classes of stocks conforms to a custom, not infrequently observed in corporation finance, of issuing bonds and preferred stock in amounts equal to the value of the tangible assets, and of issuing the common stock as a capitalization of intangible assets, such as " good-will " or " franchise value ". By requiring this additional stock to be issued without nominal value, the law attempts to compromise between the exigencies that may be thought to require stock watering and the traditional principles that demand an equality between par value and assets. *Second,* the distinction is defended on the assumption that, when stocks are preferred not only as to dividend but also as to assets in the event of dissolution, the par value is necessary in order to define the amount of this prior claim.

The first point rests on a principle of capitalization that is neither practicable nor desirable. It is not practicable because the difficulties, already noted, of securing an equality between par values and assets would remain the same even though common stock were not to be counted as a part of the total capitalization. It is not desirable because the issue of bonds and preferred stock up to the amount of the actual investment would often exceed the limits of safety for these classes of securities.

The second argument has some force but is by no means a determining consideration. Even without the device of par values, stipulation can be made as to the claim of preferred shares in the event of dissolution. To be sure, the presence of a par value gives more publicity to the amount of the claim: but that point is of no great importance.

Although the positive objections to the removal of the par value from preferred stocks are not convincing, one must concede that the reasons in its favor have less force than with common stocks. For with the former class of security, the fixed rate of dividends prevents the nominal value from influencing appreciably the market valuation. If the dividend charges are kept within safe limits, investors are not liable to be misled seriously by fictitious par values. The great danger of deception is in connection with the common stock. On the whole, however, it is probably wiser to go the whole length by removing the par value from all classes of stock.

Should it be made Compulsory?

As proposed by the Railroad Securities Commission, and as provided in all the present state laws, the issuance of no-par shares is made entirely optional with the companies. Should this continue to be the case with respect to the federal railroads, or should the change be made compulsory for all of them?

The defense of a purely optional law is that the right to issue shares of no par value is offered as a means of avoiding the necessity of issuing stock below par. Corporations may be given their choice of two practices: They may either issue no-par stock at such prices as the market justifies, or else they may retain the par value, but subject to the strict requirement that all such stock must be issued at not less than par. If they choose the latter plan, they may then be held to rigid accountability for observing the statutory requirements as to the issuance price of the stock.

But while an optional provision may be conceded to be better than no provision at all, there can be little doubt that a compulsory measure will be much more satisfactory. The advantage to be gained by the more thoroughgoing measure is the advantage of uniformity.   If some railroad companies are permitted to issue no-par stock, while other companies retain the old form of shares, confusion will result.   The success of the new system depends on the degree to which investors are educated to an appreciation of the fact that their shares represent, not a fixed amount of investment, but simply a right to a certain portion of the corporate income.   This educational process will go on much faster if the removal of the par value is made general for all railroad corporations.   Needless to say, it would go on still faster if it could be made universal for all corporations of every character.   The latter goal, however, is not apt to be reached under the divergent laws of many states — not at least for many years.   But the general adoption of the plan by all interstate railways may be secured under a law requiring federal incorporation.

Summary

The proposal to remove the par values from issues of stock is a recognition of the hopelessness of the attempt to maintain an equality between nominal capitalization and actual investment.   Several objections have been urged against the plan, but they are based, for the most part, on a mistaken or exaggerated notion of the usefulness of par values.

On the other hand, the proponents of this plan have often claimed for it too much.   They have asserted that its adoption would make all further measures of protection against stock manipulation unnecessary.   This view cannot be sustained.   The abolition of par value simply removes one source of misinformation.   It does not remove all sources; still less does it provide the necessary valuation that must take the place of the nominal capitalization.   These objects can be secured only by positive measures of financial control.

Nevertheless, the removal of par values is good as far as it goes. As applied to the railroads, the measure should be thoroughgoing; it should be compulsory rather than optional, and it should apply to stocks of all classes, common and preferred.

CHAPTER V

FEDERAL REGULATION OF RAILROAD SECURITIES

IN the preceding chapter, much emphasis was laid on the fact that the use of shares of stock without par value is not alone sufficient to meet the evils of overcapitalization, and that, in addition, there must be an effective control of security issues by the government. It remains, then, to consider in this final chapter some of the problems of government control.

Fortunately, one question that heretofore has occasioned much controversy has recently been settled: the question of state versus federal jurisdiction. Under the Transportation Act of 1920, the security issues of interstate carriers are brought under the exclusive control of the Interstate Commerce Commission. State commissions are deprived of all authority, except for their right to a hearing before the Interstate Commerce Commission in cases involving the interests of the states that they represent. So generally recognized is the wisdom of this change of jurisdiction, involving the centralization of power in the hands of one body, that we need take no time to recount the obvious advantages to be obtained.

Provisions of the Transportation Act With Respect to Control of Security Issues

Regulation of security issues is provided for in section 439 of the new Transportation Act (section 20a of the amended Interstate Commerce Act). In its general character, the measure is similar to those which have been in force for several years in the various states.[1] No carrier may issue securities without first making application to the commission and securing its consent. Exception is made of " notes to be issued by the carrier maturing not more than two years after the date thereof and aggregating (together with all other then outstanding notes of a maturity of two years or less) not more than 5 per centum of the par value of the securities of the carrier then outstanding."[2]

But the federal law gives the commission wider discretion in approving or disapproving an issue than do the laws of most states. With a few exceptions, the newer state laws enumerate certain definite purposes for which securities may properly be issued;[3] the duties of the regulating commissions are more or less restricted to seeing that the proposed issues fall within the specified purposes.[4] On the other hand, the federal statute makes no specification of purposes. It provides simply that the Interstate Commerce Commission shall approve a security issue when it finds that the issue

(a) is for some lawful object within its corporate purposes, and compatible with the public interest, which is necessary or appropriate for or consistent with the proper performance

---

[1] The most complete analysis of the different state laws is by Barron: "State Regulation of the Securities of Railroads and Public Service Companies," *Annals, Amer. Acad. Polit. and Soc. Science*, vol. lxxvi (March, 1918), pp. 167-90.

[2] Interstate Commerce Act, sec. 20a (9).

[3] New York and other states enumerate five purposes: see pp. 78-80, *supra*.

[4] But on this point commissions differ greatly in their interpretation of their powers; some, like the Wisconsin commission, interpret their powers very narrowly, while others, like the two New York commissions, assume a wide discretion. *Cf.* Ignatius, *Financing of Public Service Corporations*, pp. 290-94.

by the carrier of service to the public as a common carrier, and which will not impair its ability to perform that service, and (b) is reasonably necessary and appropriate for such purpose.

Another clause goes even further in conferring discretionary powers by authorizing the commission to prescribe the terms of an issue:

The Commission shall have power by its order to grant or deny the application as made, or to grant it in part and deny it in part, or to grant it with such modifications and upon such terms and conditions as the Commission may deem necessary or appropriate in the premises, and may from time to time, for good cause shown, make such supplemental orders in the premises as it may deem necessary or appropriate, and may by any such supplemental order modify the provisions of any previous order as to the particular purposes, uses, and extent to which, or the conditions under which, any securities so theretofore authorized or the proceeds thereof may be applied, subject always to the requirements of the foregoing paragraph.

Nothing is said in the act as to the prices at which securities may be issued. There is no prohibition of the sale of stock below par or even of the issuance of a scrip or stock dividend. In only one case is a definite statutory limit placed upon the amount of securities that may be issued; namely, in consolidations. Here the law reads that " the bonds at par of the corporation which is to become the owner of the consolidated properties, together with the outstanding capital stock at par of such corporation, shall not exceed the value of the consolidated properties as determined by the Commission." [1] No similar provision is

[1] Transportation Act, 1920, sec. 407, Interstate Commerce Act, sec. 5(6)(b).

made with respect to reorganizations, although such provisions are now commonly included in the state laws.

It is evident from the foregoing notes on the Transportation Act that Congress wished to place upon the Interstate Commerce Commission the burden of determining the principles of capitalization to which all railroads must henceforth conform. This is a heavy task. Fortunately, however, it is a task that has already been faced by the regulating commissions of more than twenty states; and their pioneer experience will serve to guide the action of the federal authorities.

Space does not permit of a discussion of all the principles that have been developed by state commissions in their control over security issues. Indeed, such a discussion has really been made unnecessary by the able studies of Barron, Bullock, Heilman, Ignatius, Ripley, and others.[1] The remainder of this chapter, therefore, will be confined to a study of three problems that seem particularly to warrant further consideration. The first topic is the control of the issuance price of shares of stock without par value; the second is the limitation of bonds and other evidences of indebtedness; the third is the treatment of security issues already outstanding.

(1) Control of the Issuance Price of Shares of Stock Without Par Value

Up to the present time, one of the chief objects of security regulation has been to prevent the practice of stock watering —that is, to prevent the issuance of shares for less than their full par value. Now, however, it is proposed to issue stock which has *no* par value. This raises a new problem. What is now to determine the prices at which shares may be is-

---

[1] See the references to these authors in the Bibliography at the end of this work.

sued? And should the government set a price limit, or should it leave this entirely to the discretion of the issuing company?

To these questions, many of the advocates of shares without par value would have a ready reply. They would insist that the removal of par values makes unnecessary any governmental control of the issuance price. This conclusion, they would say, follows from the very nature of the new kind of shares. Each share represents, not a fixed amount, but a fractional interest in the whole property. Hence, the determination of the number of shares to be issued, and of the issuance price, becomes merely a question of dividing the shares into such sizes as are most convenient to the investors. In this problem the government has no direct concern—no more than it has in the question whether or not a railway company should issue bonds in one-hundred-dollar denominations or simply in thousand-dollar denominations. In fact, the two problems are precisely the same in principle.

A similar line of reasoning would apply to the question of the propriety of a stock dividend. With par value removed, a stock dividend is supposed to mean nothing but the division of shares into smaller, more convenient claims. It does not necessarily indicate an increase in the value of the property, and therefore it need not be made contingent on such an increase.

Already, however, we have seen the weakness of this argument.[1] It assumes that the removal of par values will cause stockholders to think of their shares as representing nothing but fractional interests in the total earnings and assets of the company. But this assumption is not justified. Investors will continue to think of their shares as worth a certain relatively fixed *amount*, an amount determined in their

[1] Pp. 126-27, *supra*.

minds by the price that they paid for their holdings, by the dividend record, and by the recent market quotations. Under these circumstances, if the number of shares is increased without a corresponding increase in earning power, the investors will be influenced by their current notions as to the value of each share, and they will therefore not fully discount the reduction in the equity behind each share that is occasioned by the new issue. The result will be inflation of market values, a result which, as we saw in an earlier chapter, is responsible for most of the harm done by stock watering.[1]

The danger to which we have referred, however, applies only to *increases* of stock issue and not to original issues made at the inception of an enterprise. In the latter case there is no *established* market value by which investors may be deluded. Here, then, it will be safe for the government to allow the corporation to set its own issuance price, subject, however, to the very important condition that stock must be offered on equal terms to everyone.[2]

But with subsequent issues of stock a different rule should prevail. The government should require that the shares be sold at their full market value, or not far below it. The object of this requirement is to prevent the increase in the number of shares from being disproportionate to the increase in the earning capacity of the property. In this way the danger of inflation to which we have referred will be removed.

This rule, that shares of stock of public service corporations must be sold at their market value, has been applied

---

[1] Chap. ii, pp. 50-57.

[2] This proviso is especially necessary with respect to payment of stock to promoters. The government must set a value upon the promoter's service and must see that the amount of stock going to the promoter does not exceed his just claims for services rendered.

by some governments even where the shares are given a par value. In England the principle has been widely accepted for local public utility companies, sale at auction being a customary requirement. According to trustworthy reports, the British experience has proved highly successful.[1] In America, a similar policy has been followed by Massachusetts.[2] Here, however, the plan has met with some difficulties. During a period of falling security prices it has been impossible to obtain a ready market for shares of stock when offered at public auction or when offered to stockholders at the prevailing market prices of the old shares. On that account, the Massachusetts law was modified in 1908 so as to permit railway companies to issue shares at a price to be determined by the stockholders but subject to approval by the Railroad Commission, which must see that the price is not " so low as to be inconsistent

[1] Robert H. Whitten, *Regulation of Public Service Companies in Great Britain* (New York, 1914), ch. iii. In England the requirement that all shares of stock be sold at public auction is an integral part of the method of rate control to which local public utilities are subject. The British method, unlike the usual American method, is to base the rate of return directly on the securities rather than on the valuation of the entire property. Thus, a company may be allowed to charge rates sufficient to pay a ten-per-cent dividend on its outstanding stock. But in order to give the public the benefit of the very lowest possible rate of return on the invested capital, companies are required to sell their stocks (except the original issues) at the full market price. In this way, if a share of stock paying ten-per-cent dividends would sell for 200, the public would enjoy the use of capital at the rate of only five per cent. There is much to be said for this plan of rate regulation. Its adoption for our own railways has been advocated in a number of able articles by John Bauer; see, especially, " The Control of Return on Public Utility Investments," *Political Science Quarterly*, vol. xxxi (1916), pp. 260-88. See also Whitten, *op. cit.*, ch. xiv.

[2] See Ripley, *Railroads: Finance and Organization*, pp. 297-301; Charles J. Bullock, " Control of the Capitalization of Public Service Corporations in Massachusetts," *American Economic Association Publications*, series no. 3, vol. x (1909), pp. 384-414.

with the public interest." The commission has interpreted the above-quoted clause as requiring an issuance price " not materially lower than a price which would assure a ready market for the issue."

In view of the Massachusetts experience, it may be found advisable for the federal government to adopt a similar compromise measure permitting the issue of stock at a few points below the prevailing market prices of the old shares. Such a concession, while not ideal, would certainly create no serious danger of inflation.

If it seems wise to fix the issuance price of stock at not far below its market value, what shall we say of stock dividends? Of course, to permit stock dividends is just the reverse of requiring the sale of stock at its market value. Yet one cannot deny that a stock dividend may sometimes have a legitimate object. This object is to divide the stock into smaller shares when the value of each old share has become inconveniently large. Not only the stockholders but also the public may derive benefit from such a division; for the divided shares can be issued at higher relative prices, and consequently the cost of raising capital can be reduced. Where a case of this kind arises, permission to issue the stock dividend should probably be granted. The danger, of course, is that the increased number of shares will cause an inflation in values. But this danger can probably be minimized, although perhaps not entirely removed, by giving full publicity to the fact that the new stock does not represent any increase in actual capital.

(2) Restriction of Indebtedness

Several times in the course of this study the fact has been emphasized that overindebtedness is a menace to corporate credit of far more serious character than is an overissue of common stock. With respect to railways today, that remark is especially in point. The increasing tendency of railway companies to finance their capital requirements by the sale of bonds or notes rather than by the issuance of stock has occasioned alarm among all persons familiar with the problem. To remedy this dangerous situation by bringing about a safer balance should be one of the chief aims of government control.

How, then, is this end to be attained? The first prerequisite is a more liberal policy of rate regulation. As a result of the higher operating costs, railroads, within recent years, have suffered so severe a fall in their net earnings that they have been unable to market their stocks; they have been forced to resort almost entirely to bond issues or to note issues.

But the allowance of increased rates, necessary as it is for the purpose in question, is not enough. It will help to give railways the *power* to keep their debts within safe limits, but it may not give them the *will* to do so. Adversity, in the past, has not been the only cause of over-indebtedness; prosperity also has led to much the same result with certain railways. Some of the most reckless and fatal cases of overbonding have occurred during a period of prosperity, when speculative managements have capitalized the high earnings by inflating the funded debt as well as by watering the stock. In this way the controlling interests have been able to profit by trading on a narrower equity.[1] Two examples in recent railway history are

[1] Our American system of rate making has the unfortunate tendency to encourage this "trading on a narrow equity;" for it allows a given rate of return on the entire "fair value" of the property irrespective of the nature of the outstanding securities. For example, if the rate of return on the property value is fixed by the government at eight per cent, it will be to the interest of the stockholders to raise the largest possible amount of capital by the issuance of bonds bearing a rate of interest lower than eight per cent. The stockholders will gain the difference between the rate of interest on the bonds and the

Rock Island and Alton. In both of these instances the funded debt was increased, not to secure necessary funds for improvements, but simply to enrich the controlling stockholders.[1] These lessons of experience should not be forgotten. They prove conclusively that a mere return of " good times " will not guarantee a return of good credit; there must be safeguards against the abuse of prosperity. These safeguards must be secured by regulation.

Two very different problems are involved in the regulation of bond and note issues by the government. The one concerns the control of proposed new issues; the other concerns the treatment of issues already outstanding. In the present section we shall discuss simply the first question, leaving the matter of existing capitalization for later study.

In deciding upon a proper method of control, the federal government will naturally turn for precedents to the various states. A canvass of the states on this point discloses two divergent policies: The one policy is to set a definite statutory limit to the amount of debt that a railway company may incur; the other policy is to give to the regulating commission authority to fix such a limit as may be deemed appropriate in each individual case.

Most of the states that adopt the first policy set the limit at a certain ratio of bonds to stock, the proportion of bonds varying from two-thirds of the capital stock, as in Iowa, Nebraska, and Utah, to twice the stock, as in Delaware, Massachusetts, and Pennsylvania.[2] In many states the limit is fixed at equal portions of stocks and bonds, or of stocks and total indebtedness.

eight-per-cent return on the property. This defect of our system of rate regulation is not present in the English system, noted above (p. 138, note 1), by which the rate of return is fixed directly on the securities rather than on the valuation of the property as a whole.

[1] See pp. 55-56, *supra*.

[2] For the different state laws see Barron, *op. cit.*, pp. 176-78.

Among those states that do not fix a statutory limit, different practices prevail. The laws of several states grant to the regulating commissions specific authority to limit the proportion of bond issues. The statutes of Wisconsin and Indiana direct the commissions to fix a " reasonable proportion " of bonds to stocks, while the California law gives the Railroad Commission authority to permit bond issues equal to, in excess of, or below the amount of capital stock. In other states the laws make no reference to the restriction of indebtedness, but, nevertheless, the commissions of some of these states have interpreted their general authority to approve or disapprove security issues as giving them the power to restrict the ratio of bonds to stock.[1]

Those commissions that assume discretionary authority have generally adopted the principle that bond issues should not be permitted to exceed such limits as will give reasonable assurance that interest and discount can be met out of current earnings.[2]   Sometimes, in order to have some definite standard, commissions have fixed a proportion of bonds to stock, or of total debt to value of the property, which should ordinarily set the limit to the amount of borrowing.[3]

[1] Such was formerly the position of the two public service commissions of New York State; but several recent court decisions have thrown doubt on their authority to limit bond issues, provided that these issues are for lawful purposes: See *Re* Dry Dock, East B'way and Battery R. R. Co., 7 P. S. C. R. (1st Dist. N. Y.) 59 (1916), and *Re* Hudson River & Eastern Traction Co., 3 P. S. C. R. (2nd Dist. N. Y.) 172 (1911). On the other hand, the New Jersey commission, under a law similar to that of New York, has been upheld by the court in its assumption of control over the relative amounts of bonds and stocks: 3 Ann. Rep. N. J. P. U. C. 16 (1912) and 4 *ibid.*, 3 (1913).

[2] See, for instance, N. J. P. U. C., Conference Order No. 7 and Conference Ruling No. 13, and Cal. R. C. Rep., year ending June 30, 1913, pp. 174-75.

[3] The California commission has fixed 80% of the property value as the usual limit (*op. cit.*, p. 175); the Indiana commission will not

But such rules are not rigidly followed; they are generally waived when a company is otherwise unable to raise necessary funds.

Of the two above-mentioned policies prevailing in different states which should be adopted by the federal government—the one which provides a definite statutory limit, or the one which gives full discretion to the regulating commission? Or is some compromise measure desirable? The present Transporation Act, to be sure, seems to accept the principle of giving discretionary powers to the Interstate Commerce Commission. But this act is only an experiment; if a change is desirable, it can be made.

Each of the two policies has its own merits, and also its own shortcomings. A statutory limit has the distinct advantage of setting something definite on which a railway management may base its financial plans and on which a commission may form its decisions. The benefit of a definite guide of this kind is not to be appraised too lightly. Railway managements know what to count on; they are able to make their financial arrangements with definite knowledge of the amounts which they must raise by the sale of stock or by the reinvestment of earnings. In other words, they do not need to speculate on the uncertain outcome of a commission ruling, and, therefore, they are not tempted to gamble upon the prospects of a lenient decision forced from the commission under the plea of dire necessity.

Not only the company but also the regulating commission is in a stronger position when it is acting under a definite statutory rule. In the absence of such a rule, its position at law is somewhat precarious. Even where the law follows the example of Wisconsin and Indiana by

allow the bonds to exceed the total investment, except possibly in emergency (P. U. R. 1918 E 311); the Maine commission sets the ratio of bonds to stock at two to one (P. U. R. 1917 B 898).

granting specific power to the public service commission to fix a " reasonable proportion " of bonds to stocks, it is uncertain to what extent the courts will uphold the commission in the use of its discretion. In their solicitude for the freedom of action of the private owners and in their caution against the delegation of legislative powers, the courts may possibly put serious limits on the authority of a commission to restrict bond isssues. May they not hold that any increase in bonds must be permitted unless it is *clearly and convincingly* unreasonable? For example, would they uphold a commission if it should adopt the conservative policy of limiting bonded debt to half the value of the property? It is doubtful.

On the other hand, the principle of statutory limit has also its serious defects. Its very merit of definiteness is also its weakness. For it fails to take account of the peculiar circumstances that make each case properly a matter for separate consideration. For example, it makes no provision for emergency cases where companies lack the credit to sell stock and where they must issue more bonds or notes in order to raise necessary capital. Special treatment may be called for in such cases.

If the federal government were faced with the simple dilemma of choosing between a rigid statutory rule and the grant of full discretion to the Interstate Commerce Commission, it would probably do wisely to accept the second alternative. But is it necessary to adopt either extreme? Is there no compromise measure that will combine most of the merits of a rigid debt limit with the advantages of a flexible system? Probably there is. What is needed is a *normal* debt limit. to be set by statute, but subject to modification in cases of necessity. Such a measure would be analogous to the provisions of our present national banking law, which fixes a minimum ratio of cash reserves to deposits, but which gives to the Federal Reserve Board the power to waive the reserve requirements in cases of emergency.

Without attempting to formulate the details of this compromise measure, let us consider the general features of such a plan. First, there must be a normal debt limit. We have already noted that many of the states set this limit at a certain ratio of stocks to bonds. But a more unsatisfactory standard could hardly be suggested. No prudent investor with the slightest knowledge of corporation finance would accept the ratio of outstanding bonds to stock as even a rough measure of the solvency of a corporation. Any number of circumstances may destroy the significance of such a measure: The stock may be watered, on the one hand, or may have been issued at a premium, on the other; the bonds may bear a high or a low rate of interest; the company may have heavy fixed charges not represented by the outstanding bond issues, such as interest on floating debt, rentals of equipment or of track, amortization charges; the net earnings may be unusually low, or unusually high, as compared with the investment.

Some other test, then, should be substituted for the above-mentioned one in fixing a proper debt limit. Probably the most satisfactory one is the proportion of fixed charges to net earnings. For example, the law might provide that railroads must not incur any debt, or assume any other obligations, which would raise their total fixed charges to more than a certain percentage of the average net earnings during the preceding five-year period. Such a standard would be far superior to the current one based on the ratio of bonds to stocks. While by no means perfect, it would at least afford a rough test of safety and that is all that can be expected of any hard and fast rule.[1]

[1] Possibly a better limit than the above would be a certain ratio of

So much, then, for the statutory limit. But that limit
should be subject to relaxation in cases of necessity. Just
as the Federal Reserve Board may waive the reserve requirements of the federal reserve banks or of the member
banks, so should the Interstate Commerce Commission have
the power to make special concessions to railway companies
with respect to their debt limits. Whether or not the law
should attach certain penalties, conditions, and restrictions
to the grant of such concessions, or whether that matter
should be left entirely to the judgment and discretion of the
Interstate Commerce Commission, is a problem of detail
that need not be discussed here.

(3) Scaling Down of Existing Capitalization

Governmental regulation of railway finance labors under
the very serious handicap that it has begun late in the game.
It has come only after years of financial abuse; it takes effect when many railways are seriously overcapitalized and
when the majority of railways are overindebted. Until
this situation is remedied, until the weaker roads are compelled to readjust their outstanding obligations so as to
make their capital charges commensurate with their earnings, it will avail little to attempt to regulate future security
issues. One cannot build solidly except on a solid base.

What, then, is to be done at this late hour? Should there
be a drastic and immediate scaling down of excessive capitalization, or should the readjustment be moderate and
gradual? In either case, how is the end to be attained?

Fortunately, one of the problems that have hitherto
caused much difficulty in financial reorganizations need
give but little concern in the present instance; namely, the

total expenses (operating expenses, taxes, and fixed charges) to gross
earnings. *Cf.* Lawrence Chamberlain, *The Principles of Bond Investment*, 3d ed. (New York, 1913), pp. 276-78.

problem of reducing the total capitalization of a company so as to make it correspond to the assets. That difficulty is disposed of by the conversion of all outstanding shares of stock into shares without par value. The removal of the par values will minimize the necessity of any reduction in the number of shares held by present stockholders.

But a far more difficult and important problem remains in the necessity of cutting down the fixed charges of over-indebted railway companies. For it cannot be too frequently emphasized that overindebtedness, rather than over-capitalization in the ordinary sense of the term, is the incubus on American railways today.

If constitutional difficulties were not in the way, a strong case could be made for a federal statute requiring all over-indebted companies to reorganize at once on a sound financial basis. Such a law would seem harsh to existing investors; yet it might be justified in the public interest. And even the investors might ultimately gain rather than lose, as they would be required merely to exchange bonds and notes for stock without yielding their right to whatever earnings the valuation of the property may entitle them to receive.

But we hardly need argue the merits and demerits of such a law; for it would almost certainly be held unconstitutional. There is, to be sure, a possibility that a reorganization of the kind mentioned might be upheld in court if it were made an incidental feature of an act requiring the consolidation of all interstate carriers into a few large companies under federal charter. But even that procedure would be of doubtful constitutionality.

These same constitutional difficulties have been met by the various state commissions in their attempts to regulate public utility securities. With two or three exceptions, therefore, the state commissions have not attempted to scale down capitalization already outstanding but have con-

fined themselves to the supervision of new security issues.[1]
Gradually, it is hoped, this moderate policy will bring the
companies to a healthy financial condition—in some cases
through the reinvestment of earnings or the increment of
property values, in other cases through bankruptcy, receivership, and reorganization.

Whatever one may think of the ultimate possibilities of
this Fabian method, one must admit that it is woefully
slow. As to a gradual readjustment through the investment of earnings, that is the very thing that a financially
weak company cannot do. It has no surplus to invest.
Only strong companies, like the Pennsylvania Railroad, can
be counted on to turn back large earnings into their property.
As to bankruptcy and reorganization, that may be deferred
indefinitely. By skimping maintenance charges and by
making no extensions and improvements, an overbonded
company may keep up a miserable existence for years without becoming formally bankrupt. Meanwhile, of course,
the public suffers from poor service.

Not all states, however, have been content to leave existing security issues alone. Massachusetts and Texas are
notable exceptions. These states have adopted the policy
of refusing to sanction new security issues whenever the
proposed issue would bring the total capitalization out of
proportion to the property values. Under this rule, an
overcapitalized company is compelled to scale down its outstanding securities before it may make any further issues.

In the execution of this general policy, the methods of
Massachusetts and of Texas differ materially. The practice of Massachusetts is determined by precedents set by

[1] See Heilman, "The Development by Commissions of the Principles of Public Utility Capitalization," *Journal of Political Economy*,
vol. xxiii (1915), pp. 888-92; Ignatius. *Financing of Public Service
Corporations*, pp. 294-96.

the regulating commissions; that of Texas is determined by statute. Consequently, the rule has been applied less rigidly in the former state than in the latter.

With what success have these efforts met? Are the results sufficiently satisfactory to warrant imitation by the federal government? Judging from the experience of Massachusetts, one might conclude that the experiment is successful, at least with respect to gas and electric companies. For Massachusetts is probably the only state in which the local public utilities are, for the most part, conservatively capitalized. Yet Massachusetts really furnishes no adequate test. In that state, regulation began before overcapitalization had become prevalent. Therefore, the problem of scaling down existing security issues has not been a serious one.

The case of Texas, however, is quite different. When Texas first undertook the regulation of railroad securities, overcapitalization had already been carried to absurd extremes. The famous Stock and Bond law of 1893 was a belated attempt to cure the evil. According to that law, railroad companies are forbidden to issue bonds in excess of the " reasonable value " of their property as determined by the Railroad Commission, except that in emergencies railroads may be allowed to issue stocks and bonds which, together, will not exceed the property value by more than fifty per cent.

Most writers agree that the results of this law of 1893 have not been satisfactory.[1] To be sure, the statute has led to a material reduction in capitalization; but it has also acted as a serious check to the raising of new capital.

[1] For discussions of security regulation in Texas see Ripley, *Railroads: Finance and Organization*, pp. 301-6, and articles listed in the Bibliography, *infra*, under the names, R. C. Duff, Lewis H. Haney, E. T. Miller, Charles S. Potts, *Railway and Engineering Review*, Edward P. Ripley, and R. A. Thompson.

Rather than submit to a reduction of their outstanding security issues, railway companies have simply avoided making new issues.

Recognition of the unfortunate tendency of the Stock and Bond law to check investment has caused the Texas legislature to modify the provisions considerably. It is now provided that a railway may issue new securities for extensions and for double-tracking, regardless of the amount of capitalization already outstanding. No doubt these modifications have helped to remove the check to the raising of new capital, but they have done so simply by a surrender of the very principle on which the original act was based.[1]

It must be admitted, then, that the experience of Texas in its attempt to scale down redundant security issues is not such as to invite imitation by the federal government. But are we to conclude that the task of readjusting existing capital burdens is hopeless, and that the wiser course is to follow the precedent set by the other states in taking account only of *future* security issues? This conclusion does not follow. The fatal defect of the Texas plan is that it applies the pressure in the wrong place. The only punishment meted out to companies for failure to scale down excessive capitalization is refusal to permit them to issue further securities. But this is a punishment that hurts the public more than the company. What is needed is some form of governmental action that will induce financially weak companies to reorganize, but which will not give them the alternative of remaining unregenerate simply by declining to apply for permission to issue new securites. How is this end to be accomplished?

The means to this end are to be found in a wise exercise of the powers of government over railway rates and railway

[1] See pp. 92-93, *supra.*

service. These powers may be exercised in such a way as to compel or induce overbonded, miscapitalized companies to submit to reorganization. Compulsion may be used by a policy of severity toward the companies that fail to reorganize; persuasion, by a policy of liberality toward those companies that make the necessary capital readjustments.

There are numerous measures by which this policy of discrimination can be enforced. Rate control furnishes one possibility. It is a well recognized fact that the government enjoys a considerable latitude in its power to fix rates. The courts, to be sure, will protect a railway in its right to a "reasonable return on the fair value of the property." But the rate of return that the courts uphold as "reasonable" is the minimum rate—a rate usually considerably below that which is required in order to maintain the credit of the railway company. Suppose, now, that Congress were to fix a minimum rate, just high enough to satisfy the courts in their protection of property rights, which every railway is to be permitted to earn. Suppose further, that it sets a higher rate of return, which may be earned only by those railways that conform to certain standards of proper capitalization—standards based, perhaps, on the relation of fixed charges and preferred dividends to the valuation of the property. The application of this differential rate will hasten the reorganization of financially top-heavy railways, either through voluntary action on the part of security holders or through bankruptcy and foreclosure proceedings.

The use of the rate-making power may be supplemented by other forms of pressure. Service requirements may be enforced without leniency. Weak railways are frequently able to postpone bankruptcy only by allowing their service to deteriorate. If required to improve their service, to establish grade crossings, to replace worn-out rails, and to purchase new equipment, they would be forced quickly into a receivership. Now the government, within limits, has the power to enforce reasonable service standards. Especially where the safety of the traveling public is at stake, its authority has been upheld in court. Let the government enforce these standards rigorously, and let the railways take the consequences if their financial structure makes it impossible for them to fulfill their obligations as public servants.

It must be admitted that the policy suggested above—the policy of forcing hopelessly overcapitalized railway companies to submit at the earliest possible moment to a thoroughgoing readjustment—breaks violently with the tendency of the past and with notions current at the present time. Hitherto, it seems generally to have been assumed that leniency rather than rigor is properly to be shown to financially weak railway companies. Instead of hastening a receivership and reorganization, the effort has been to avoid it. This has been notably the case with the New England railways; forbearance has marked the treatment of these mismanaged companies. Laws have been passed validating previous illegal acts and permitting new corporate action otherwise forbidden by statute. Everything has been done that could well be done to forestall the threatened bankruptcy.

This past practice of tempering the wind to the shorn lamb may or may not have been wise. Certainly bankruptcy and receivership are unfortunate occurrences, unfortunate both to the public and to the private investors. But one must admit that the situation today is unusual. We have come to a crisis in our railway affairs. Railway credit must be revived, and revived at once. At a time like this, stronger medicine is required than may have seemed necessary in the past. Measures that once might have seemed too radical are now the only alternatives to the *more* radical step of government ownership and operation.

So far we have emphasized the wisdom of reversing the present policy of leniency toward miscapitalized railways. Equally essential, however, is the adoption of a liberal policy toward those companies that are willing to cooperate with the government in putting themselves on a sound financial footing. To state the case more concretely, the holders of junior bonds or notes in an overindebted railway should be induced to exchange their loans for shares of stock, not merely by the threat of loss in case the exchange is not made, but also by the prospect of a liberal return if the conversion is accepted.

After all, no policy of governmental control of securities can do much to restore railway credit unless it is accompanied by a policy of rate control that will make the stock holdings of *properly financed railways* an attractive form of investment. To that end, a dividend rate should be allowed that is sufficiently above the current yield of bonds to compensate for the extra risk. If the public is unwilling to grant that extra rate, if it begrudges more than a " savings-bank rate " of interest, it would better proceed without delay to adopt a program of government ownership; for under these conditions, private ownership is bound to fail.

Summary

The Transportation Act of 1920, in its provisions for federal control of railway securities, follows the main outlines of the more recent public utilities laws of the various states. It differs, however, from most of these laws in giving to the regulating commission the widest discretionary powers instead of making specific rules on which decisions must be based.

Among the many problems that will arise under the new

plan of financial regulation, three are of special importance:
(1) the control of the issuance price of stock where the
shares are without par value; (2) the restriction of indebtedness; (3) the treatment of security issues already outstanding.

The first problem raises the question whether or not the
removal of the par value from shares of stock makes it unnecessary for the government to control the issuance price.
To this question the proper answer seems to be that the
price of an *initial* issue of shares may safely be left to the
discretion of the directors, but that *subsequent* issues should
be required to be sold at not far below the full market value.
This latter requirement is for the purpose of preventing the
speculative inflation that often results from the issuance of
shares to stockholders at an unduly low price.

The second problem concerns the limit that should be
placed on the power of a railway corporation to incur debts.
On this point two distinct policies have prevailed in different states: The one policy is to fix a statutory limit, usually
a certain ratio of bonds to stock; the other policy is to give
the regulating commission authority to set such limits as it
may deem appropriate to the particular circumstances. This
chapter proposes a compromise. Let a definite *normal* debt
limit be fixed by statute, but let the Interstate Commerce
Commission have the authority to set aside this limit whenever circumstances require. The statutory limit, however,
should not be the one now prevailing in the different states.
Instead of setting a proportion of bonds to stock, the law
should fix a *normal* ratio of fixed charges to net earnings.
The latter ratio is much superior to the former as a test
of the solvency of a railway corporation.

The third problem—treatment of existing security issues
—is the most puzzling of all. Both constitutional and
practical difficulties are present. Under ordinary circum-

stances, therefore, one might be inclined to leave outstanding securities alone. Indeed, most of the states have done just that. But railway credit, today, is in such a critical condition that a more radical policy is called for. There must be a speedy reorganization of grossly overbonded railways in order to leave a clean sheet for sound financial practices in the future. The government, therefore, should use all legitimate means in its power to hasten such reorganizations. This end may be accomplished by adopting a policy of severity toward recalcitrant companies and a policy of liberality toward those companies that conform to the standards of sound capitalization.

APPENDIX A

Court and Commission Decisions on the Relation of Capitalization to " Fair Value "

THERE is no present occasion to cite at length the decisions on this subject, in view of the excellent digests that are already available.[1] It is sufficient to summarize the situation, and to present some points of interpretation which may not have been fully discussed elsewhere.

I. The Courts

In a legal discussion of the relation of capitalization to fair rates, the famous dictum in Smyth v. Ames[2] is the starting point. This dictum, which has already been quoted,[3] mentions " the amount and market value of its stocks and bonds " as one of the elements to be considered in determining the " fair value " of a public service company. Does this mean that the amount of the securities must be considered, even if it is known to exceed the actual cost of the property? That question is answered in the Smyth decision as follows:[4]

If a railroad corporation has bonded its property for an amount that exceeds its fair value, or if its capitalization is

---

[1] Whitten, *Valuation of Public Service Corporation*, vol. i, Index *s. v.* "Capitalization," vol. ii, pp. 874-92; Beale & Wyman, *Railroad Rate Regulation*, 2nd ed., 1915, pp. 220-229.

[2] 169 U. S. 466 (1898).

[3] Pp. 21-22, *supra*.

[4] *Ibid.*, p. 544.

156

largely fictitious, it may not impose upon the public the burden of such increased rates as may be required for the purpose of realizing profits upon such excessive valuation or fictitious capitalization; and the apparent value of the property and franchises used by the corporation, as represented by its stocks, bonds, and obligations, is not alone to be considered when determining the rates that may be reasonably charged. . . .

It must be conceded that even this statement is not quite as clear-cut a disavowal of the right to earn a return on watered securities as might be desired: it still leaves the feeling that perhaps such securities are entitled to a *little* consideration, although not to very much. But the course of subsequent court decisions, including that of the Supreme Court itself in Knoxville *v.* Knoxville Water Co.,[1] leaves little doubt in the matter. In the Knoxville case the court said:

Counsel for the Company urge rather faintly, that the capitalization of the Company ought to have some influence in the case in determining the valuation of the property. It is a sufficient answer to this contention that the capitalization is shown to be considerably in excess of any valuation testified to by any witness, or which can be arrived at by any process of reasoning.

Other courts, both state and federal, have uniformly followed these precedents, denying the right to a return on excessive securities. Whitten, Beale, and Wyman cite numerous examples.

II. *The State Public Service Commissions*

The various state public utility commissions are almost unanimous in declaring that capitalization, when determined without governmental approval, shall not be made a

[1] 212 U. S. 1, 11 (1909).

basis of valuation. Only one partial exception has come to the writer's attention; namely, that of the Maryland Public Service Commission, which considers itself bound by a peculiar clause in the public service law of the state to protect "as far as possible" the value of the bonds issued prior to the act.[1] With respect to stock issues, the Maryland commission follows the practice of other states in assuming to disregard par values.

In order to conform to the letter of the Smyth *v.* Ames decision, which requires that the amount and market value of the stocks and bonds be considered, the customary procedure of the commissions has been to take evidence on the capitalization and on the return on securities. But if capitalization is found to be excessive, the statement is usually made that the commission has "considered" the amount of the stocks and bonds, and has determined that it should be disregarded, or given little weight, in fixing a rate.[2]

[1] Bachrach *v.* Consolidated Gas, Electric Light and Power Co. of Baltimore, Ann. Rep. Md. P. S. C., 1913, p. 39.

[2] Whitten, vol. ii, p. 874-92, cites decisions of various public service commissions with respect to capitalization as a factor in "fair value." More recent cases are: City of Lincoln *v.* Lincoln Water & Lt. Co. (Ill. P. U. C.), P. U. R. 1917 B 1; *Re* Richmond Lt., Heat & P. Co. (Ind. P. S. C.), P. U. R. 1917 B 300; *Re* Kansas City Elec. Lt. Co. (Mo. P. S. C.), P. U. R. 1917 C 728; *Re* Newton Gas & Elec. Co. (N. J. P. U. C.), P. U. R. 1916 A 514; Moretz *v.* Edison Elec. Illum. Co. of B'klyn, 7 P. S. C. R. (1st Dist. N. Y.) 175; Ben Avon Borough *v.* Ohio Valley Water Co. (Pa. P. S. C.), P. U. R. 1917 C 390; *Re* Portland Ry., Lt. & P. Co. (Ore. P. S. C.), P. U. R. 1918 B 266. In a review of the above-cited New York case, Dr. John Bauer, referring to the question whether capitalization should be considered in fixing a "fair value," remarks: "The point involved, so far as the writer knows, was never before so definitely set forth and argued by a company; and the commission's view may therefore serve as a leading and commendable precedent" (*American Economic Review*, vol. vii [1917], pp. 438-42).

III. *The Interstate Commerce Commission*

Of particular significance is the attitude of the Interstate
Commerce Commission. One of the well-known rate decisions of this body is sometimes quoted as giving recognition to
capitalization even when it is clearly shown to be fictitious.
This was the Spokane case of 1909,[1] in which complainants
against the railways made the plea that thirty million dollars of the capitalization of the Great Northern represented
no investment in the property and hence should not be considered in determining a fair rate of return. To this contention, Commissioner Prouty, in the ruling decision, replied as follows:[2]

But we very much doubt whether in determining what rate
of dividend the stock of a railway company may earn we can
properly deduct in every instance watered stock. It is impossible to distinguish the spurious from the genuine. Those
who received their stock without consideration have usually
parted with it and that very stock, if it could be identified, is
owned by its present possessor for a valuable consideration.
The whole stock has gone upon the market, has assumed a
market value, has become the subject of investment by innocent stockholders. We may undoubtedly and we should
have in mind the manner in which this stock was issued and
the consideration which was paid for it, but we do not think
that we should, for example, treat the outstanding stock of
the Great Northern as $120,000,000 and not $150,000,000.
These transactions ought to have been prevented to begin with.
Great sums might have been properly saved the public by
suitable supervision at the outset, but the evil has been done,
and for the most part cannot be safely undone. If this government in the past has permitted the "capitalization" of
earnings and securities and the "conferring of benefits" it
ought not to-day to penalize the innocent holders of the values
thus created.

[1] 15 I. C. C. Rep. 376.
[2] *Ibid.*, p. 410.

The above quotation, however, is purely in the nature
of a dictum, as the commission decided to require the reduction in rates without reference to this particular point
at issue. The same question was discussed in the ruling
opinion by Commissioner Prouty in the Eastern Rate Case
of 1911.[1] Referring there to the Smyth *v.* Ames dictum
that the amount and market value of the securities should
be considered, Mr. Prouty remarked that, although counsel
did not mention these matters, the commission regarded
them as entitled to consideration. But in the further discussion of this point, he seems to indicate that it is *market*
value rather than *par* value which may constitute a claim
for protection. In this case, as in the Spokane cases, the
question of capitalization had no effect on the actual decision; for it was held that in any event, no justification could
be found for the proposed increase in rates.

These two opinions of Mr. Prouty, in so far as they may
be interpreted as indicating a recognition of watered securities in the determination of a fair return, have found no
acceptance in the later decisions of the commission. In the
Western Rate Advance Case of 1911,[2] which was decided
on the same date as the above-mentioned Eastern case,
Commissioner Lane remarked in the ruling opinion that
"this commission cannot accept capitalization as representing either investment or value." In Railroad Commission
of Texas *v.* Atcheson, Topeka, & Santa Fe Railway Co.,
et al.,[3] decided in the same year, Commissioner Harlan said,

The capitalized value per mile of road is not to be regarded,
however, as having any significance in this controversy, nor do
we attach any weight to the book value appearing on the accounts of the Company.

[1] 20 I. C. C. Rep. 243.
[2] 20 I. C. C. Rep. 307, 320.
[3] 20 I. C. C. Rep. 463, 474.

In an express rate decision of 1912,[1] Commissioner Lane made the following statement:

There is no sacredness in the stated amount of the capital stock of any company. When the courts speak of a return upon the capital of a public utility they mean a return upon the investment. The investor in a railroad, an express company, or a telegraph company should be compensated for the sacrifice that he has made and not paid a premium because of the manner in which he chooses to state his financial condition or his expectations.

In the more recent rate-advance cases, the commission's treatment of capitalization has been clear and consistent. The amounts of outstanding securities have been considered simply as *evidence* of the actual investment in the physical property. For instance, in the Five Per Cent Case of 1914, the commission based its conclusion that the returns were inadequate on the showing that the ratio of net operating income to book values had declined since 1900. The validity of the book values themselves, as indication of true value, was expressly denied. But it was believed that the comparative statements would give at least a rough indication of *relative* investments during the period in question.

The same use of capitalization as an indication of real values has been followed in the other cases, but always with the attempt to distinguish the fictitious from the genuine.[3]

[1] 24 I. C. C. Rep. 421.

[2] 31 I. C. C. Rep. 351, Reopened, 32 *Ibid.*, 325.

[3] Western Rate Advance Case, 35 I. C. C. Rep. 497 (1915); Anthracite Coal Rate Case, 35 I. C. C. Rep. 220 (1915); Fifteen Per Cent Case, 45 I. C. C. Rep. 57 (1917).

APPENDIX B

Protection of Credit as a Factor in Commission Rate Decisions

In Chapter I the point was made that commissions sometimes allow more than a " fair " rate of return in order to bolster the credit of weak public service corporations. To the extent that this is true, overcapitalization may result in the allowance of excessive charges. We shall here consider, first, the position of the Interstate Commerce Commission and, second, the attitude of various state commissions. The courts may be left out of account, as they generally assume no authority beyond the guaranty of " fair " returns.

I. The Interstate Commerce Commission

In all the general rate-advance cases before this commission, the carriers have urged a declining railway credit as the chief reason for raising rates. As Commissioner Lane put it, in the Western Rate Advance decision of 1911,[1] the main contention of the carriers was that " we need the money." In so far as this need for higher rates in order to maintain credit may be due to unavoidably rising costs of capital, or to higher operating expenses, the commission has always recognized the plea as valid. But where the weakness of credit is attributable to overcapitalization, or to other causes for which the railways themselves are responsible, the argument has not been accepted so readily.

In the Eastern Rate Advance Case of 1911,[2] it was urged

[1] 20 I. C. C. Rep. 307.
[2] 20 I. C. C. Rep. 243.

by the carriers that their rates were insufficient to maintain their credit. This fact was denied in the decision, but even if it were admitted, the commission did not consider itself at liberty to allow higher rates on that account. In the majority opinion, Commissioner Prouty remarked :[1]

A fundamental economic fallacy underlies the proposition that we should permit rates otherwise unreasonable for the purpose of bolstering up the credit of our railways. It would be much better for the government to guarantee these bonds than to permit the people and the industries of this country to bear the burden of unreasonable transportation charges.

A similar view was expressed in the first decision on the Five Per Cent Case of 1914.[2] In this case the carriers held that rates were insufficient either to yield a " fair return " on the property or to attract capital. The commission stated that it was deluged with letters from all over the country pleading the need for higher rates in order to raise credit to stimulate business. But it held that, even if it had the will, it did not possess the power to raise rates for this purpose. As to the necessities of the weak railways, it said :[3]

No one could reasonably contend that the public should pay higher transportation rates because once prosperous properties—like the New Haven, the Chicago & Eastern Illinois, the Alton, and the Frisco, or the Cincinnati, Hamilton & Dayton—may now be in need of additional funds as a consequence of mismanagement.

The commission, however, did concede the need for increased revenues, although not on the grounds mentioned

[1] *Ibid.*, p. 253.
[2] 31 I. C. C. Rep. 351.
[3] *Ibid.*, p. 358.

above.   At the first hearings, the five-per-cent increase was permitted only within the Central Freight Association and not for the entire Official Classification Territory.   But the case was later reopened,[1] and a more general increase was allowed on the ground that the earnings of recent months had declined.   While the new decision makes no overt admission that the commission had changed its position with respect to the question of credit, Commissioner Clements, in his dissenting opinion, complained that in fact this plea of the carriers was heeded.   After referring to the weight that the majority seemed to place on the book values, which were obviously untrustworthy, he said:[2]

If, now, to strengthen and maintain the credit of the carriers, regardless of the causes of its exhaustion or impairment, and without the application of the usual tests of reasonableness, these increases are justified, then, it seems to me that we are only at the beginning of what I fear will be a train of demoralizing results, disappointing and embarrassing to all concerned.   It is by no means certain that it would not, in the long run, be cheaper to the public to guarantee the bonds of the weak roads unable to meet their obligations, rather than to try to take care of them by increased rates, which inure to the strong roads as well as to the weak.

This view of Mr. Clements, that the commission was influenced by the argument of the need to strengthen credit, seems to find support in the Fifteen Per Cent Case of 1917.[3] It will be recalled that in this case the railways urged the existence of a dire emergency due to the war.   Rising costs, it was claimed, were threatening earnings at the very time when the railways must go into the market for large funds in order to provide facilities required by the war.   In its

[1] 32 I. C. C. Rep. 325 (1914).
[2] *Ibid.*, p. 340.
[3] 45 I. C. C. Rep. 303.

decision, the commission admitted a need for higher earnings and allowed certain increases, although it did not find that
any such emergency existed as would justify the immediate
general increase desired by the carriers. Certainly, in this
case, the main consideration was that of the expediency of the
increase rather than the question of fairness to investors.
It is of course quite possible that in this case the commission
may have considered the two questions to be identical, or
at least indistinguishable. But the fact that attention was
directed primarily to need rather than to justice is significant. This position was taken even more unequivocally in
the concurring opinion of Commissioner Harlan.[1]

Up to the present, then, the position of the Interstate Commerce Commission with respect to credit requirements as a
separate factor in rate making must be considered somewhat
uncertain. *Formally* it is still on record as denying the
claim; *practically* it seems recently to have given it recognition.[2]

II. *State Public Service Commissions*

The Massachusetts Public Service Commission has taken
a position similar to that of the Interstate Commerce Commission, denying its own authority to sanction " unreasonable " rates in order to support railway credit. In its annual report for 1916 it made the following remarks under
the heading, " the Question of Credit : "[3]

Beyond question the great need at the present time of most

---

[1] *Ibid.*, p. 326.

[2] The Transportation Act of 1920 provides that the Interstate Commerce Commission, in determining a " fair return " on the property
value, " shall give due consideration, among other things, to the transportation needs of the country and the necessity (under honest, efficient
and economical management of existing transportation facilities) of
enlarging such facilities in order to provide the people of the United
States with adequate transportation " (Sec. 422).

[3] 4 Ann. Rep. Mass. P. S. C. xxv.

of the steam railroads and street railways operating within the Commonwealth is new capital. . . . In view of this situation, many have felt that the Commission, in dealing with questions of rates or service, ought to be guided chiefly by its concepts of what will do the most at the moment to promote the sale of the companies' securities.

While this feeling is not unnatural, it is the product of a one-sided point of view, and disregards the fact that the Commission exercises no arbitrary power nor unfettered discretion, but is the administrator of a definite code of laws by which its action must be governed. . . .

It is quite possible that in certain cases an increase in rates, though inherently unjust and unreasonable, may be expedient as the lesser of two evils, but this is a broad question of *policy,* which the legislature must decide in any given case, and which has not been left to the discretion of this Commission.

Not all commissions, however, have accepted this view of their duties in rate making. The Maryland Public Service Commission seems to have taken a different position in the case of Bachrach *v.* Consolidated Gas, Electric Light & Power Co. of Baltimore.[1] This company had been heavily overcapitalized as a result of consolidation; capitalization was $43,518,088, of which $29,358,000 consisted of bonds and other debt, while replacement cost depreciated was estimated at perhaps $26,417,414, including five million dollars for value of easements. Referring to the question of a proper rate of return, the commission expressed itself as follows:

Whatever is done now must bear fruit in the future. The citizens of Baltimore are dependent upon the Defendant Company for two of the prime necessities of modern life, and its extension to meet the growing demand for its products is one

[1] Report for year 1913, p. 39.

of the conditions upon which the growth of the city and the
multiplication and development of its industries depends. That
the sins of over-capitalization impose a burden upon the people
is undeniably true, and they cannot be too strongly condemned.
But the burden would not be lightened, but made heavier, if
conditions should be imposed upon the present management
of the Company, which is not responsible for the things that
we complain of, which would seriously impair its ability to
meet the just demands of the community for service.[1]

The rates which the commission finally fixed were estimated to be sufficient to yield a return of over $500,000 after
payment of interest charges.   In arriving at this " reasonable return " the commission considered itself under obligation to protect the interest of the bonds pursuant to a
peculiar statute of the state mentioned in Appendix A.   But,
in addition, it allowed an estimated surplus sufficient to pay
preferred dividends and to leave a small balance, in order
to support the company's credit.

The California Railroad Commission, according to the
testimony of one of its former members, has sometimes been
compelled to allow higher rates in order to support the credit
of a weak company.   In a report before the National Association of Railway Commissioners in 1913, the late Commissioner Eshleman of California made a statement to this
effect and gave it as evidence of the need for security regulation.[2]

Since our entry into the war, the need to support the
credit of public utilities has been more generally recognized
by the various state commissions.   Thus, the Indiana commission recently remarked that while a company must bear
its part of the war burden, it must nevertheless be kept in a

[1] *Ibid.,* p. 54.

[2] *Proceedings of the Twenty-fifth Convention of the National Association of Railway Commissioners,* 1913, p. 195.

state of financial solvency.[1]   The California commission
said that "in determining the rate of return . . . careful
consideration must be given, among other matters, to the
ability of the utility to secure additional funds necessary for
extensions, betterments, and improvements."[2]   The New
York Commission for the Second District[3] permitted a
company to earn rates sufficient for an extension of credit
under the rules imposed by the War Finance Corporation.
The commissions of Pennsylvania,[4] Maine,[5] and Oregon[6]
are on record as giving consideration to financial needs.

The New Jersey Commission[7] has gone so far in its effort to support public utility credit as to allow the Public
Service Electric Company to increase rates during the war
so as to pay eight-per-cent dividends after all fixed charges,
although no appraisal of the plant had been made.   In its
decision, it said:

We have not dealt with the value of the property in this
proceeding.   In the existing emergency, the determining consideration must be to keep the property in uninterrupted and
effective operation.   This involves the payment of fixed rentals and charges without regard to the value of property, since
failure to ratify such contractual rents and charges would
jeopardize uninterrupted operation.

[1] *Re* Fisher, P. U. R. 1918 F 662.
[2] *Re* San Joaquin Lt. & P. Corp., P. U. R. 1918 F 662.
[3] *Re* Empire Gas & Elec. Co., P. U. R. 1918 D 912.
[4] *Re* Springfield Consol. Water Co., P. U. R. 1918 E 358.
[5] *Re* Lewiston, Augusta & Waterville St. Ry., P. U. R. 1918 E 681.
[6] Littlepage *v.* Mosier Valley Teleg. Co., P. U. R. 1918 E 425.
[7] *Re* Public Service Electric Co., P. U. R. 1918 B 857.

APPENDIX C

The Alton Controversy

Perhaps no other recent instance of stock watering has received so much attention, or has been the subject of such division of opinion, as the Alton recapitalization accomplished under the leadership of Mr. Harriman. Condemned by one writer as combining "practically all of the possible abuses or frauds" of railway finance,[1] it has been defended by another as a perfectly innocent and proper procedure,[2] while a third holds that "actual damage was done to the company's credit, but no harm was done, or could possibly have been done, to the travelling public."[3] In 1907 the case was investigated by the Interstate Commerce Commission, which reported in terms of sharpest condemnation.[4] More recently, the matter has again been brought to public attention by the controversy between Professor Ripley, who supports the Interstate Commerce Commission in its criticism, and Mr. George Kennan, who stoutly defends Mr. Harriman's acts as above reproach.[5] The points

---

[1] Ripley, *Railroads: Finance and Organization*, p. 262.

[2] Kennan, see references below.

[3] *Railway Age Gazette*, editorial comment, "'Cost of Service' and the Alton Case," vol. xlviii (1910), p. 222.

[4] 12 I. C. C. Rep. 295 (1907).

[5] Ripley, *op. cit.*, pp. 262-7; Kennan, "The Chicago and Alton Case: A Misunderstood Transaction," *North American Review*, vol. cciii (1916), pp. 35-54; Ripley, "Federal Financial Regulation," *ibid.*, pp. 538-52; Kennan, "Misrepresentation in Railroad Affairs," *ibid.*, pp. 871-82. Both of Mr. Kennan's articles have appeared, in revised and amplified form, in separate monographs bearing the above titles (The Country Life Press, Garden City, N. Y., 1916).

at issue in this controversy touch so closely upon the principles developed in the early chapters of this treatise, that it will be worth while to review them in detail.   First, however, let us note briefly the conceded facts of the case.

The Facts of the Case

At the end of the last century, the Alton was a conservatively capitalized railway with a low indebtedness, making excellent earnings and paying from seven to eight per cent dividends.   But its management under President Blackstone was not sufficiently progressive.   It had failed to keep pace with the modern development of transportation facilities and had not even provided adequate allowances for maintenance and depreciation.   This fact, together with a reduction in freight rates under increasingly keen competition, had been responsible for a decline in net earnings during the 90's, with a consequent reduction in dividends from 8 per cent to $7\frac{1}{2}$ per cent and then to 7 per cent.

In 1899, Mr. Harriman and his associates secured control through the purchase of nearly all the common and preferred stocks at 175 and 200, respectively.   Their announced policy was to make such improvements as would put the road in first-class condition, and to develop the line as a connecting link in the larger Harriman system.   To a measurable extent, both of these policies were carried out. But the financial transactions involved in the program for development were made the occasion for an increase in capitalization far beyond the amount required in order to secure the necessary funds.   This inflation was accomplished by the following series of steps.

First Step, 1899.   Sale of thirty-two million dollars, face value, of three-per-cent bonds to stockholders—the syndicate—at sixty-five.   These bonds were later resold by the syndicate at a very material profit.   The average price ob-

tained has never been made public, although the Interstate
Commerce Commission reported that ten million dollars of
the bonds were bought at ninety-six by New York life-
insurance companies.   According to an estimate of the commission, the average price was ninety, which would give a
profit of eight millions; but this figure has been challenged
by Mr. Harriman's protagonists.

Second step, 1900. Payment of a thirty-per-cent extra cash
dividend on both classes of stock, amounting to $6,669,000.
The funds for the dividend were secured from the
proceeds of the above-mentioned bond issue.   This left only
$13,410,000 from the issue of thirty-two millions of bonds
available for refunding and improvements.

In order to prevent the resulting excess of nineteen millions in capital liabilities from creating a deficit on the
balance sheet, the assets of the company were written up by
$12,444,177.66, with a corresponding credit to " Construc-
tion Expenditures Uncapitalized."   Against the latter account were charged the thirty-five-per-cent discount on the
bonds and the cash dividend.   This left a debit balance
which was transferred to Profit and Loss.   The syndicate
justified this procedure on the ground that a surplus of over
twelve millions had been accumulated by the reinvestment
of earnings, but that this surplus had not, heretofore, appeared on the books, owing to the practice of charging improvements to Operation instead of to Capital.   Under that
interpretation, the bonds that were issued in excess of the
additions to property would amount simply to a capitalization of the surplus.

Third step, 1900. Formation of the Chicago and Alton
Railway, as a holding company to take over the stock of the
operating railroad.   The reason given by the syndicate for
the formation of this new company was that the charter of
the old company would not permit the merger of some newly

acquired lines. Exchange of securities was made on the following terms: For $3,472,200 par value of the old preferred, the holding company paid ten million dollars in cash; for $18,322,400 par value of the old common, the holding company issued $19,489,000 of its own preferred stock and $19,542,800 common stock.

In order to raise the ten millions of cash in payment for the preferred stock of the railroad, and also to secure an additional three millions for the purchase of a branch line owned by the Harriman syndicate, the railway company sold to its stockholders (composed almost entirely of the members of the syndicate) twenty-two million dollars, face value, of 3½-per-cent collateral trust bonds, at 60, netting the company about thirteen million dollars. As in the case of the earlier bond issue, these securities were issued much below the market price, which ranged from 78 to 86½ for two or three years after the issue. Another source of profit to the stockholders was thus tapped.

Fourth and last step, 1906. The holding company and the operating company were consolidated to form the new Chicago and Alton Railroad. In this case there was no material increase of capitalization, the exchange of stocks being on the basis of par for par, except for the issuance of $879,300 " prior lien and participating " stock to take up the small outside holdings of the original railroad stocks on the basis of three new shares to one of old preferred, and two to one of common. This step has not been the subject of special criticism.

The total effect of these various financial transactions may be seen in the following table, which compares the liabilities of the old railroad in 1898 with those of the consolidated company in 1906.

Liabilities	Year 1898	Year 1906	Increase	Per cent Inc.
Common Stock	$18,751,100	$19,542,800	$ 791,700	4
Pfd. & Prior L. Stocks ..	3,479,500	20,423,300	16,943,800	480
Total Share Capital ...	$22,230,600	$39,966,100	$17,735,500	80%
Funded Debt Outstdg. ..	8,650,850	64,350,000	55,699,150	644
Guaranteed Stocks	2,129,000	3,693,200	1,564,200	73
Other Liabilities	940,957	5,865,056	4,924,099	525
Total Indebtedness	$11,720,807	$73,908,256	$62,187,449	530%
Total Liabilities	$33,951,407	$113,874,356	$79,922,949	235%

Against this increase in total capitalization of about eighty million dollars was an additional investment in the property, according to the company's own books, of only eighteen million dollars.

Changes in Control of the Railway

Since the time of this financial reorganization, there has been frequent shift in the controlling interests of the railroad. In 1904, the company came under the joint control of the Union Pacific and the Rock Island railroads, the former having purchased a majority of the Alton preferred stock, and the latter owning some of the preferred and nearly all of the common.[1] This arrangement lasted only until 1907, when the "Clover Leaf" (Toledo, St. Louis & Western Railway), a Hawley property, secured control through the purchase of the Rock Island's interest. The Union Pacific still retained, and continues to retain, its holdings of about ten million dollars of the preferred, but it did not remain in

[1] The Interstate Commerce Commission states that the Rock Island, between 1903 and 1907, purchased $4,880,000 of the preferred and $14,420,000 of the common at a total cost of $9,709,876.49. In 1907 it sold all of this common and $4,100,000 of the preferred to the "Clover Leaf" line in exchange for $4,110,000 series "A" bonds of the latter road (for the preferred stock) and $5,047,000 series "B" bonds (for the common stock). 36 I. C. C. Rep. 43 (1915).

control after 1907; so that Mr. Harriman's connections
were severed at that time.   More recently, since both the
Alton and the Clover Leaf roads have got into financial difficulties, the Union Pacific interests have again assumed
direction.

Rise and Fall of the Income

So much for the financial circumstances and the changes
in control.   Now for the effects on the well-being of the
railroad.   Under the Harriman management, the physical
condition of the road was materially improved.   Gross earnings per mile increased 56 per cent from 1899 to 1907;
net earnings per mile increased 55 per cent.   This rise took
place in spite of material reductions in rates.   In 1907, the
income after payment of the heavy fixed charges was sufficent to pay the 4-per-cent preferred dividend, with a surplus
of about 5 per cent on the common stock.   When Mr. Harriman severed his connections with the road, in that same
year, he seemed to have left it in a condition of prosperity.
Current issues of railway and financial journals, commenting on the remarkable growth of traffic, cited the case as
another instance of the effects of Mr. Harriman's golden
touch.

But beginning with the year 1908, the Alton record has
been almost steadily downward.   To be sure, gross earnings
have continued to increase with the exception of a few off-
years.   Net earnings per mile, however, reached a limit in
1909 which was never exceeded or even again attained
until 1917, under the extraordinary war conditions.   At
the same time that income was falling off, fixed charges were
steadily rising.   In 1912, there was a deficit after payment
of interest, and this has continued during every subsequent
year.   Were it not for the financial support of the Union
Pacific, which has advanced the necessary funds, the Alton
would in all probability have become a bankrupt road.

Professor Ripley's Criticisms

Professor Ripley places the responsibility for the recent misfortunes of the Alton squarely upon the Harriman reorganization.   By that act, he says, the road was overloaded with a burden of fixed charges in excess of earnings. As a result, it has been unable to secure money for necessary improvements, its service has deteriorated, and it faces the "need of high rates for service in order to support the fraudulent capitalization."

Mr. Ripley lays great emphasis on the alleged attempt on the part of the promoters to conceal the fictitious nature of the increased capitalization by devious accounting methods —by writing up the assets and charging the 30-per-cent cash dividend and the bond discount to the resulting surplus, and by using the holding-company device in order to conceal the financial position of the operating company.

Mr. Kennan's Reply

In his reply, Mr. Kennan admits the facts of the fictitious increase in capitalization, but insists that the transactions were entirely legitimate, that they were not concealed, and that they resulted in no injury to the company.   The chief points in his attack on Mr. Ripley's argument may be stated and examined in turn.

1. That the syndicate did not make exorbitant profits. Professor Ripley's estimate of $23.600,000 profits is grossly exaggerated.   While it is impossible to tell the exact amount of the gain, the prices at which the syndicate sold their securities would give them "a net profit of probably eight per cent and possibly twelve or fifteen per cent upon the cash outlay." (p. 41) [1]

Ans. The estimate of profits is wholly speculative.   The actual figures have never been divulged, and the quoted

[1] Page references are to *North American Review*, vol. cciii (1916).

market prices of some of the securities in question are only nominal. To be on the safe side, Mr. Kennan's estimate is not challenged.

2. That the creation of the surplus was entirely legal and proper. Legal authority supports the right of companies to charge to capital bona-fide improvements that have previously been charged to operating expenses. (pp. 43-4).

Ans. In a revised edition of his article, Mr. Kennan himself admits by implication that the surplus was not justified. He there says:

The only reasonable objections to such a course are stated, very fairly, by Professor Mead and President Fink. The former is of opinion that capitalization of sums previously spent for betterments is justifiable only when the betterments have actually increased earnings, which in the Chicago and Alton case they had not done. "Its earnings for many years," Professor Mead says, "had been stationary, and its property had not been kept up to standard." If the company had maintained a proper depreciation account, there would have been no such surplus. For these reasons he disapproves of the capitalization of past betterments and the issue of bonds to pay a dividend thereon; but he admits that, in the absence of state legislation expressly forbidding it, "the legality of the proceeding is not to be questioned." This judgment, however, does not change the facts that the money was expended, and the cost might properly have been charged, at the time, to capital account. The proceeding involves a question of financial expediency, but not, in any sense, of illegality.[1]

In the present discussion, the question of legality is of little concern: we are here studying the principles, not the existing laws, of capitalization. But it may be noted in passing that even the legality may be questioned if it is true, as the above quotation indicates, that "if the company had

[1] *The Chicago and Alton Case* (Garden City, N. Y., 1916), pp. 23-4.

maintained a proper depreciation account, there would have been no such surplus." Much more important, however, is the undeniable fact that the procedure was financially inexpedient and therefore contrary to public policy.

3. That the payment of the thirty-per-cent cash dividend and the sale of bonds to reimburse the treasury for the payment were legal and proper. They amounted simply to the capitalization of the above-mentioned surplus. (pp. 43-4).

Ans. Assuming the validity of the surplus,—a very questionable assumption,—the issuance of bonds against it was probably legal under the state laws as they then stood. But that it was in violation of the public interest is entirely clear. Any increase in debt weakens the corporate credit by reducing the margin of safety. It is therefore justified only as a means of securing capital that cannot be secured on equally good terms by the sale of stock. In the case at hand no such necessity prevailed, for no capital whatever was raised. The same remark applies to the issuance of bonds by the holding company in place of the preferred stock of the operating company. The added burden of fixed charges brought no compensating advantage to the railway. From the public standpoint it was therefore unjustifiable.

During recent years, railway officials have constantly urged the necessity of higher earnings in order to enable the roads to secure capital by the sale of stock instead of bonds. What, then, shall we say of a railroad that makes its very prosperity the excuse for assuming heavy and wholly unnecessary increases in bonded debt?

4. That the sale of bonds at 65 was reasonable under the circumstances. While it is true that the Harriman syndicate made a large profit by reselling at a higher price, the excessive amount of the profit could not have been anticipated. It was due partly to the passage of a New York

law making the bonds a legal investment for savings banks, and partly to the unexpectedly favorable conditions of the market. A few years later, in 1907, the prices of these bonds had fallen almost to the issuance price, although they were " just as good then as they ever had been." (pp. 44-6).

Ans. This argument might have more weight were it not for the fact that the syndicate repeated the trick soon afterwards by causing the holding company to issue its $3\frac{1}{2}$-percent collateral trust bonds at 60. The market prices of these bonds ranged from 78 to $86\frac{1}{2}$ for two or three years after the issue.

5. The alleged overcapitalization. Those who make that charge do so on the assumption that capitalization should represent the actual cost. But there is good authority for the position that capitalization should be based, not on cost, but on earning power. The latter is the more defensible standard. (p. 46 [1]).

Ans. The earning-power basis is discussed at length in Chapter III of this study.[2] It rests on the false notion that capitalization should represent value, but it cannot be sustained even on that theory, except in so far as it happens to coincide with market value. The extended defense of the principle presented in Mr. Kennan's revised edition[3] illustrates both of these fallacies: First, it assumes that capitalization should be based on value and hence that the only question is to find out what that value is; second, it assumes that a fair measure of value is the probable earnings *capitalized at hypothetical rates of interest*. In defense of this latter view, Mr. Kennan makes the following quotation from a well-known economist:

[1] More fully developed in the revised article printed in monograph form: *The Chicago and Alton Case*, pp. 28-32.

[2] *Supra*, pp. 82-88.

[3] *Op. cit.*

As an investment, land is valued, as is any other form of income-producing property, by capitalizing its annual return at the current rate of interest.[1]

Now this assertion is perfectly sound; but one notes that the author was careful to state that the capitalization is " at the *current* rate of interest "—current, that is, for similar investments at that particular time.   Mr. Kennan, however, in his computation of earning power, uses rates very different from the current ones.   He calculates on the basis of the 3 and 3½-per-cent nominal rate of interest on the bonds, the 4-per-cent dividend on the preferred stock, and a four-per-cent rate on the common.[2]   No one of these rates was as high as the market rate; that is to say, every one of these securities was selling well below par.   Therefore, one cannot accept a capitalization based on those rates as representing in any way " the value of the property."[3]

6. That, accepting earning power as the proper standard, the Alton capitalization was not excessive.   Mr. Harriman estimated that, as a result of certain improvements of the physical property, net earnings would rise to four million dollars per year, sufficient to pay interest on the bonds and dividends on both classes of stock.   The actual results more than justified this estimate.   In 1907, net earnings were

[1] H. R. Seager, *Principles of Economics* (New York, 1913), p. 239.
[2] *Op. cit.*, p. 34.
[3] If the present discussion were an attempt to determine whether, and to what extent, Mr. Harriman and his associates were guilty of a breach of business ethics, it would be necessary to add to the above criticism this statement: that in spite of the scientific absurdity of the earning-power theory of capitalization, it is a principle that has been accepted by many persons of high standing and honorable reputation. The real defense would therefore be, not that Mr. Harriman's methods were valid, but that they conformed to the standards of the time. But the matter of personal blame does not concern the present discussion.

$4,415,974—enough to cover all prior charges plus five per cent on the common stock (pp. 47-8).

Ans. Even on the basis of earning power, the capitaliza-tion was excessive. The apparent large earnings during the last year of the Harriman control were not a fair test. This point is discussed in the section following.

7. That the later misfortunes of the Alton road were in no sense caused by Mr. Harriman's management; for they did not take place until Mr. Harriman had left control. They were due to a number of circumstances—to poor business conditions, to the unexpected rise in operating ex-penses, to the decline in rates, and to the inefficient financial management by the " Clover Leaf " interests. " Mr. Har-riman left the road on a dividend paying basis in 1907 and two years later he died." (pp. 49, 873).

Ans. It is true that the trouble *did not appear* until after Mr. Harriman's withdrawal from control. But that does not absolve his syndicate from responsibility. Anyone who will consult the successive operating reports of the railway during the period in question will note that the factors in the railway's financial misfortunes are two: first, an extra-ordinary upward trend in the fixed charges from the begin-ning of the Harriman administration down to the present time; second, a decline in net earnings after 1909. Either of these two trends alone would have meant an injury to the railway credit; but the serious condition—the failure to earn interest charges—was due to the combination of the two.

The changes in earnings and fixed charges may be noted in the table below, which gives the figures on a per-mile basis.

CHICAGO & ALTON RAILROAD. INCOME AND CHARGES PER MILE OF LINE
OPERATED, BY THREE YEAR AVERAGES [1]

	1897-9 Blackstone Period	1905-7 Harriman Period	1912-14 Clover Leaf Period
Gross Oper. Revenue	$8,266	$12,680	$14,246
Maintenance	1,506	3,035	5,219
Other Expenses & Taxes	3,750	5,529	6,898
Oper. Expenses & Taxes	5,256	8,564	12,117
Net Earnings	3,010	4,116	2,129
Other Income	296	45	85
Total Net Income	3,306	4,161	2,214
Fixed Charges	1,267	2,603	3,816
Dividends	1,865	847	0
Surplus	174	711	* 1,602

* Deficit

| Mileage .... | 844 | 915-970-970 | 1026-1026-1033 |

[1] The figures for the three different periods are not strictly comparable owing to changes in the accounting methods; but for practical purposes the discrepancies are not serious. Prior to 1899, the company deducted certain expenses before stating the gross operating revenues; but in 1899 and thereafter these charges were added to operating expenses instead of being deducted before stating the gross. In its operating report for 1899, the company computed the 1898 earnings on the new basis as well as on the old. I have therefore used the new basis for 1898 and have also estimated the 1897 earnings on the new basis, by adding to the reported gross earnings and to the operating expenses the amount ($460,970) by which the 1898 earnings as computed by the new method exceeded the earnings as computed by the old method. By the same method, I have estimated the maintenance charges for 1897 at $90,408 in excess of the reported figure.

"Fixed charges" include interest on debt, discount charges, dividends on guaranteed securities, rentals of leased lines.

For the first period, the figures have been computed from the annual reports of the company; for the two later periods, they have been taken from *Moody's Analyses of Railroad Investments*, with a modification by which taxes are included in operating expenses rather than in fixed charges.

(a) The increase in fixed charges. For this extraordinary increase the Harriman reorganization is admittedly in large measure responsible. Even the rise that took place after 1907 must be attributed in part to this circumstance; for the recapitalization placed such a burden of debt upon the company that it was unable to secure the necessary funds except by borrowing on unfavorable terms.

(b) The decline in the net earnings. This was due chiefly to the increased operating expenses. Other factors mentioned by Mr. Kennan were also in part responsible.

But is it really true, as Mr. Kennan suggests, that when Mr. Harriman left the road, the earnings were sufficient to justify the inflated capitalization? According to the operating statement, they were indeed sufficient to pay four or five per cent on the common stock. But aside from the fact that the two years which gave this favorable showing were unusually good years for the road (1905 the St. Louis Fair, 1907 the high business prosperity), one may question whether the amount of the net earnings was not deceptive. For the experience of later years shows that during the Harriman period, maintenance charges were inadequate. Let us look further into the matter.

The reader will note from the above table that the chief reason for the decline in net earnings during the " Clover Leaf " period has been the extraordinary rise in maintenance charges. During the first three years of its control, the new management had allowed the charges to drop off; but beginning with 1911 it raised them above any previous amounts. Under the Harriman control, the average maintenance charges per mile, from 1900 to 1907, were $2,595; under the Clover Leaf, the average from 1908 to 1917 was $4,422, an increase of $1,827 or seventy per cent. This rise is all the more extraordinary in view of the fact that even in the Harriman period, maintenance charges had

risen to over twice the figure under the Blackstone administration. In 1899, for example, the maintenance charges
were only $1,481 as compared with $3,120 in 1907.

It is evident from these facts that the Alton railway was
left by the Blackstone administration in a much worse
physical condition than was at first supposed. Even the
increased maintenance during the Harriman period did not
suffice to make good the deferred charges of prior years.
This view is confirmed in the annual report of the President
for 1913, which states that the property was still in poor
physical condition as a result of the previous insufficient
provisions for upkeep.[1]

We are compelled, therefore, to conclude that, if the
Alton earnings during the last years of Mr. Harriman's
control had been made to bear their fair share of the maintenance charges, they would not have yielded the amounts
required to support the high capitalization.[2] When, in addition, one recalls that no attempt was made to amortize the
heavy bond discounts, and that consequently this burden has
been deferred to the time when the bonds mature, it is
evident that the apparent prosperity of the Alton in 1907
was an illusion.

8. That the transactions, so far from being concealed,
were given complete publicity. They were without exception announced in the current financial publications.
Therefore, by no chance could investors have been deceived. (pp. 51-2; 877-9).

Ans. It is probably true that Mr. Harriman met all *formal*
requirements of publicity. Each step in the reorganization
was published at the time. The Interstate Commerce report, on which Mr. Ripley based his statement to the con-

[1] *Report*, p. 6.

[2] This statement is not meant to imply that Mr. Harriman designedly
skimped the maintenance charges in order to conceal the true condition.
It is quite possible that the inadequacy of the charges did not become
apparent until later.

trary, did an injustice to Mr. Harriman by failing to make this fact clear.

But it is also necessary to remark that the public notices of the transactions, though they may have conformed to the customary requirements, were wholly insufficient to protect investors against the deceptive appearances of the transactions. The various steps in the financing were so complicated, and the accounting methods so involved, that the successive public announcements were sure to confuse the ordinary investor. Take, for example, the procedure of setting up a surplus against which to charge the discount on the bonds and the extra cash dividend. It is true that an experienced analyst or accountant, by comparing the balance sheets and earnings statements for succeeding years, and by consulting the notices of the financial transactions in the current financial journals, could arrive at the true position of the assets and liabilities. But most investors are not experienced in analysing reports and cannot take the time to make critical examinations. These people would almost surely be deceived by the appearance of a great increase in the investment.

9. That Professor Ripley's accusation that Mr. Harriman prejudiced the interests of shippers " by creating the need for high rates for service in order to support the fraudulent capitalization " is doubly misleading: It indicates, first, that rates are dependent on capitalization, and second, that Mr. Harriman raised rates to bolster up fictitious securities. The former is an economic fallacy; the latter is simply a misstatement of facts, for rates actually declined after the reorganization.

Ans. (a) The relation of capitalization to rates has been discussed in Chapter I of this study. There it is shown that the connection is by no means fanciful, but that the more serious charge against overcapitalization is that it injures railway service.

(b) It is apparently true that rates fell instead of rising. That was due largely to competition, and perhaps partly to state regulation. If Professor Ripley understood the contrary, he was misinformed. *But if one takes his words literally, they are perfectly true.* The Alton reorganization, by injuring the company's credit, has certainly " created the need for high rates of service in order to support the fraudulent capitalization." To be sure, this need has not yet been satisfied. But are not railway spokesmen constantly telling us that in the future, the salvation of the transportation service of the country depends on securing some method of rate control which will enable the *weak roads* to earn sufficient profits? And has not the Alton become one of those weak roads that demand special tenderness?

10. " The most surprising of all Professor Ripley's misstatements is that which charges Mr. Harriman with ' crippling ' the Alton road ' physically.' " As a matter of fact, so far from crippling it, he built it up. When he bought it, it was a run-down, old-fashioned railway; when he left it, it was a first-class, modern system.

Ans. No one can deny that Mr. Harriman made conspicuous improvements. It is true that a large amount of deferred maintenance had not been made good when he left control. Nevertheless, the physical condition was immensely improved.

But this accomplishment, however creditable, does not belie the charge that great harm was done by the financial reorganization. These two preformances were entirely separate, and the latter was not a necessary means of accomplishing the former. Mr. Harriman's management therefore did two things—it improved the road physically, and it injured its credit. The latter circumstance made it impossible for the new administration to maintain the very standards of physical efficiency that Mr. Harriman had himself inaugurated.

APPENDIX D

BIBLIOGRAPHY ON THE REGULATION OF THE SECURITY
ISSUES OF RAILROADS AND OTHER UTILITIES

Consideration of space has required the restriction of this list to references that touch directly on the subject of security regulation; hence the omission of many of the other references that have appeared in the footnotes of this study. The preparation of this bibliography has been much facilitated by the typewritten *List of References on Regulation of the Issuance of Railroad Stocks and Bonds,* prepared by the Bureau of Railway Economics in Washington, and dated January 12, 1919. The last-named list contains about fifty references that are not mentioned below, either because they did not seem of sufficient importance, or because they do not bear directly on the subject, or else because they were not accessible to the present writer.

Andrews, Edward L., " The President's Proposal for a Federal Railway System." *Albany Law Journal,* vol. lxix (1907), pp. 266-71.

Atwood, Albert W., " Protecting the Stockholder. Part IV: By Law." *Harper's Weekly,* vol. lviii, Feb. 28, 1914, pp. 28-31.

Ayres, Arthur U., " Governmental Regulation of Security Issues." *Political Science Quarterly,* vol. xxviii (1913), pp. 586-92.

Barron, Mary L., " State Regulation of the Securities of Railroads and Public Service Companies." *Annals of the American Academy of Political and Social Science,* vol. lxxvi (March, 1918), pp. 167-90.

Bauer, John, " The Control of Return on Public Utility Investments." *Political Science Quarterly,* vol. xxxi (1916), pp. 260-88.

——, " The Brooklyn Edison Case Decided." *American Economic Review,* vol. vii (1917), pp. 438-42.

 Capitalization not a factor in value for rate making.

Beale, Joseph H. & Wyman, Bruce, *Railroad Rate Regulation,* 2d ed. by Bruce Wyman. New York, 1915. Ch. vi, " Basis of Capital Charges," Topic B, " Outstanding Capitalization."

Birdseye, Cumming & Gilbert, editors, *Annotated Consolidated Laws of the State of New York,* 2d ed. New York, 1918. Abstracts of court and commission decisions on the Public Service Commissions Law of New York, relative to control of capitalization, vol. vi, pp. 6914-21, 6939-44, 7104-05.

Bullock, Charles J., "Control of the Capitalization of Public Service Corporations in Massachusetts." *American Economic Association Publications*, series no. 3, vol. x (1909), pp. 384-414. Discussion, pp. 415-30.

Calkins, Grosvenor, "Massachusetts Anti-Stock-Watering Law." *Quarterly Journal of Economics*, vol. xxii (1908), pp. 640-45.

Chamber of Commerce of the United States of America, *Referendum No. 21 on the Report of the Railroad Committee on Questions of Railroad Regulation. Washington, D. C., September 12, 1917.*

Clements, Judson C., "Public Control of Railway Capitalization." *Railway Age Gazette*, vol. lix (1915), pp. 1227-8.

Cleveland, Frederick A. & Powell, F. W., *Railroad Finance*. New York, 1912.

Commercial and Financial Chronicle, "Financial Government by Commission," vol. lxxxvii (1908), pp. 1391-2.

——, Editorial on decision of New York Court of Appeals in the Delaware and Hudson case, vol. lxxxix (1909), pp. 1504-5.

Dawes, Rufus C., "Regulation of Utility Corporations: Criticism of Commission Control in Limiting Capitalization and Stock Issue on Public Service Properties." *Public Service*, vol. ix (1910), pp. 78-80.

Duff, R. C., *The Attitude of the Texas Banker to Texas Railroads.* Houston, 1911. Reprinted from *Texas Bankers' Journal*, April, 1911.

Dunn, Samuel O., *The American Transportation Question*. New York, 1912. Pp. 258-67, "Regulation of Finances."

——, *Regulation of Railways*. New York, 1918. Ch. viii, "Regulation of Securities."

Electric Railway Journal, "New York Public Service Commission's Report to Legislature," vol. xxxiii (1909), pp. 133-7.

——, "Attitude of Massachusetts Commission on Questions Affecting Capitalization," vol. xxxiii (1909), p. 339.

——, "Consolidated Stock Not Limited by Fair Value," vol. xlviii (1916), pp. 965-7.
    Discusses a decision of the Illinois Public Service Commission.

Electrical World, "Issuance of Stock for Purposes of Consolidation," vol. lxviii (1916), pp. 266-8.
    Discusses a decision of the Illinois Public Service Commission.

Erickson, Halfred, *Regulation of Public Utilities: Three Discussions*. Madison, Wis., 1911. Pt. iii, "Government Regulation of Security Issues."

——, "Should Government Regulate Security Issues of Public Utilities?" *Public Service*, vol. xiii (1912), pp. 115-21.

Escher, Franklin, "The Hadley Report's Bearing on Railroad Investments." *Harper's Weekly*, vol. lvi, Jan. 6, 1912, pp. 28-9.

——, "The Problem of the Railways. V. Proposed Federal Control of Railway Security Issues." *Harper's Weekly*, vol. lvi, Sept. 28, 1912, p. 22.

Eshleman, John M., "Should the Public Utilities Commission Have Power to Control the Issuance of Securities?" *Annals of the American Academy of Political and Social Science*, vol. liii (May, 1914), pp. 148-61.

Farwell, F. C., "Why Railroad Financing in Iowa is Difficult." *Electric Railway Journal*, vol. xxxix (1912), pp. 696-7.

Fink, Henry, *Federal Regulation of Railroad Securities and Valuation of Railroad Properties. Letter to the Railroad Securities Commission in Reply to Request for Information and Opinions, New York, December 31, 1910.* Roanoke, Va., 1911(?).

Gardiner, W. H., Jr., *The London Sliding Scale as a Method for the Government Regulation of Public Service Corporations. Read before the National Electric Light Association at its Twenty-First Convention, held at Atlantic City, New Jersey, June 5, 6, 7 and 8, 1906.* New York, 1906. Appendix A, "The Public Regulation of Gas Companies in Great Britain and Ireland, with Special Reference to the 'Sliding Scale,'" by Nathan Matthews. Appendix B, "An Act to Consolidate and Convert the Capital of the Gas Light and Coke Company of London, England."

Geisse, H. L., "Attitude of Wisconsin Commission on Security Issues." *Electric Railway Journal*, vol. xlvii (1916), pp. 602-3.

Gerstenberg, Charles W., *Materials of Corporation Finance.* 3rd ed. New York, 1915.
    Many valuable reprints on security regulation and capitalization.

Gray, John H., "Competition and Capitalization, as Controlled by the Massachusetts Gas Commission." *Quarterly Journal of Economics*, vol. xv (1901), pp. 254-76.

Haines, Henry S., *Problems in Railway Regulation.* New York, 1911. Ch. viii, "Problems in Finance."

Haney, Lewis H., ed., *Some Corporation and Taxation Problems of the State.* Bulletin of the University of Texas, no. 236, Austin, 1912. "Railway Capitalization," by Judge N. A. Stedman, pp. 83-92. "Railway Capitalization in Texas," by R. F. Higgins, pp. 93-110. "Railway Capitalization and the Valuations of the Texas Commission," by Judge W. D. Williams, pp. 111-120.

Heilman, Ralph E., "Two Rate Decisions of Importance." *Quarterly Journal of Economics*, vol. xxix (1915), pp. 840-8.
    Discusses the Middlesex and Boston Rate Case.

——, "The Development by Commissions of the Principles of Public Utility Capitalization." *Journal of Political Economy*, vol. xxiii (1915), pp. 888-909.

——, "Commission Control of Refunding Utility Securities." *Utilities Magazine*, vol. i, March, 1916, pp. 26-30.

——, "The Control of Interstate Utility Capitalization by State Commissions." *Journal of Political Economy*, vol. xxiv (1916), pp. 474-88.

——, "Capitalization of Public Utility Consolidations." *American Economic Review*, vol. vii (1917), pp. 187-94.

Higgins, R. F., see Haney, Lewis H., ed.

Hines, Walker D., *Statement of Walker D. Hines before Railroad Securities Commission at New York, December 22, 1910.* New York, 1910 (?).

Holmes, Fred L., *Regulation of Railroads and Public Utilities in Wisconsin.* New York, 1915. Ch. xvi, "Regulation of Stocks and Bonds."

Ignatius, Milton B., *The Financing of Public Service Corporations.* New York, 1918.

Johnson, Emory R., "Regulation of Railroad Securities." *Investment Weekly*, vol. xix (1917), pp. 14-15.

Journal of Commerce (New York). Editorials on federal regulation of railway securities. Nov. 5, 1913, p. 8; May 9, 1914, p. 4; May 21, 1914, p. 4; June 22, 1914, p. 4; June 30, 1914, p. 4; July 24, 1914, p. 4; Nov. 5, 1915, p. 4.

Knox, Philander C., "The People, the Railroads, and the National Authority." *Albany Law Journal*, vol. lxx (1908), pp. 144-49 (147-48).

La Follette, Robert M., "Let Us Reason Together." Editorial, *La Follette's Weekly*, vol. vi, no. 5 (January 31, 1914), pp. 1-3. Opposes security regulation.

Lane, Franklin K., "Railroad Capitalization and Federal Regulation." *American Review of Reviews*, vol. xxxvii (1908), pp. 711-14.

Lawton, W. H., "Government Regulation of Securities." *Journal of Accountancy*, vol. xii (1911), pp. 357-60.

Literary Digest, "Fatherly Guidance for Railroad Financiers," vol. xlviii (1910), pp. 49-50.

Lovett, Robert S., *Statement of R. S. Lovett before the Railroad Securities Commission. (As rearranged and amplified.) . . . December 21, 1910.* New York, 1911 (?).

Lyon, Hastings, *Corporation Finance.* Boston, 1916.

Massachusetts, *Report of the Commission on Commerce and Industry, March, 1908.* Boston, 1908. Pp. 57-69, "Massachusetts Statute Regulating the Issue of New Stock by the Public-Service Corporations."

——, *Report of the Special Commission to Investigate Voluntary Associations, Boston, January 4, 1913.* House no. 1788.

——, *Information Relative to Voluntary Associations Owning or Controlling Public Service Corporations.* Public Document, no. 101. Boston, 1913.

——, *Report of Tax Commission on Voluntary Associations, Boston, January 17, 1912.* House no. 1646.

Matthews, Nathan, see Gardiner, W. H., Jr.

Mead, Edward S., *Corporation Finance.* Rev. ed. New York, 1915. Ch. vi, " State Supervision of Securities."

——, " The Public Service Commission and the Investor." *Lippincott's Monthly Magazine,* vol. xc (1912), pp. 764-8.

Miller, E. T., " The Texas Stock and Bond Law and Its Administration," *Quarterly Journal of Economics,* vol. xxii (1907), pp. 109-19.

Moody's Magazine, " Government Regulation of Bond and Stock Issue," vol. xi (1911), pp. 53-4.

Morris, Ray, *Railroad Administration.* New York, 1920. On security regulation, see pp. 215-23.

Mulvey, Thomas, Under Secretary of State of the Dominion of Canada, *Company Capitalization Control. Report on Existing Legislation in Canada and Elsewhere.* Ottawa, 1913.

——, " Certified Securities." *American Economic Review,* vol. iv (1914), pp. 588-601.

——, " Blue Sky Law." *Canadian Law Times,* vol. xxxvi (1916), pp. 37-45.

National Association of Railway Commissioners, *Proceedings,* 1889-1918. Most of the recent numbers contain discussions of security regulation. See, esp., *Proceedings of 25th Annual Convention* (1913), and of *28th Annual Convention* (1916).

National Civic Federation, *Commission Regulation of Public Utilities; a Compilation and Analysis of Laws of Forty-Three States and of the Federal Government, for the Regulation by Central Commissions of Railroads and Other Public Utilities.* New York, 1913. Pp. 849-906, " Stock and Bond Issues."

——, *Draft Bill for the Regulation of Public Utilities With Documents Relating Thereto. Authorized to be Published by the National Civic Federation, October 23, 1914.* New York, 1914.

" Newlands Committee," *Hearings.* See United States Congress, Joint Committee on Interstate and Foreign Commerce.

Potts, Charles S., *Railroad Transportation in Texas.* Bulletin of the University of Texas, no. 119, March 1, 1909. Ch. ix, " Control of Capitalization—the Stock and Bond Law."

——, " Texas Stock and Bond Law." *Annals of the American Academy of Political and Social Science,* vol. liii (May, 1914), pp. 162-71.

Public Service, " Ohio Utility Commission is Criticized by Financiers," vol. xiii (1912), p. 70.

Railway Age Gazette [Nearly every volume of recent years contains discussions of railroad security regulation.]

——, " Many Railway Presidents Favor Federal Supervision of Securities," vol. lvi (1914), p. 39.

——, "Regulation of Railway Securities," vol. lvi (1914), pp. 61-2.

Railway and Engineering Review, " The Effect of regulation in Texas," vol. lii (1912), pp. 493-95.

Railway World, " To Regulate the Issuance of Railway Securities," vol. lviii (1914), pp. 345-47.

Ramstedt, A. P., Extracts of letter of A. P. Ramstedt, Chairman of the Public Utilities Commission of Idaho, on the subject of Railway Regulation, addressed to Senator Newlands. *Railway Age Gazette*, vol. lxi (1916), p. 1134.

Rea, Samuel, *Reprint of Letter to Railroad Securities Commission, February 6, 1911*. Philadelphia(?), 1911.

Reynolds, C. A., " Overcapitalization of Public Utilities." *Case and Comment*, vol. xxi (1915), pp. 875-77.

Ripley, Edward P., *Address before the Texas Welfare Commission, Austin, May 21, 1912*. Subject, " Railroads and Railroad Securities in Texas."

Ripley, William Z., *Railroads: Rates and Regulation*. New York, 1913. Review of the Report of the Railroad Securities Commission, pp. 573-78.

> Substantially a reprint of an article in the *American Economic Review*, mentioned below.

——, *Railroads: Finance and Organization*. New York, 1915. Ch. ix, " State Regulation of Security Issues."

——, " The Capitalization of Public Service Corporations." *Quarterly Journal of Economics*, vol. xv (1901), pp. 106-37. Reprinted in *Trusts, Pools and Corporations*, 1st ed. (Boston, 1905), ch. vii.

——, " Railroad Valuation." *Political Science Quarterly*, vol. xxii (1907), pp. 577-610.

——, " Report of the Railroad Securities Commission." *American Economic Review*, vol. ii (1912), pp. 181-85.

——, " One Law Instead of Forty-Eight." *New York Times Annalist*, vol. iii (1914), pp. 588-89.

——, " Public Regulation of Railroad Issues." *American Economic Review*, vol. iv (1914), pp 541-64.

> Substantially reprinted as ch. ix in *Railroads: Finance and Organization*.

Sinsheimer, Paul, " Financial Aspects of Valuation." *Utilities Magazine*, vol. i, Nov., 1915, pp. 165-69.

Smalley, Harrison S., " The Regulation of Railway Capitalization." *Editorial Review*, vol. iv (1911), pp. 275-86.

Spencer, Arthur M., " The Prevention of Stock-Watering by Public Service Corporations." *Journal of Political Economy*, vol. xiv (1906), pp. 542-52.

Stedman, Judge N. A., see Haney, Lewis H., ed.

Stiles, Meredith, N., "Problems of the Railroad Securities Commission." *Moody's Magazine*, vol. xi (1911), pp. 167-72.

Stoddard, W. L., "Possible Railway Securities Legislation." *Railway Age Gazette*, vol. lix (1915), p. 946.

——, "The Securities Bill Side-Tracked." *Railway Age Gazette*, vol. lx (1916), p. 154.

Taft, William Howard, President, *Presidential Message of January 7, 1910*, Cong. Rec., vol. xlv, p. 461 *et seq.*
    Recommends federal control of railroad securities.

Thelen, Max, "The Newlands Railroad Investigation." *Utilities Magazine*, vol. ii, Jan., 1917, pp. 1-9. Reprinted in the *Hearings* of the "Newlands Committee," pp. 1069-78.

——, "Federal Incorporation of Railroads." *Utilities Magazine*, vol. ii, March, 1917, pp. 1-11. Reprinted in the *Hearings* of the "Newlands Committee," pp. 1085-94.

——, "Desirable Scope and Method of Federal Regulation of Railroad Securities." *Annals of the American Academy of Political and Social Science*, vol. lxxvi (March, 1918), pp. 191-201.

Thompson, R. A., "Regulation of the Issuance of Texas Railroad Securities by the State Government." Address before the Texas Academy of Science at Austin, October 24, 1902. *Transactions* of the Academy for 1902, pp. 1-17.

——, "Methods Used by the Railroad Commission of Texas under the Stock and Bond Law, in Valuing Railroad Properties." *Transactions of the American Society of Civil Engineers*, vol. lii (1904), pp. 328-45. Discussion, pp. 346-64.

Trumbull, Frank, *Statement of Mr. Frank Trumbull, Chairman of the Board of Directors of the Chesapeake and Ohio Railway Company, before the Federal Railroad Securities Commission at New York, December 22, 1910.* (*Revised.*) New York(?), 1910.

United States. Congress. House. Committee on Interstate and Foreign Commerce.
    Hearings ... on H. R. 6268 to Limit the Issue of Stocks and Bonds. [May 12, 1908]. Washington, 1908.
    Hearings before the Committee ... on Bills Affecting Interstate Commerce. [Jan. 18-March 25, 1910]. Washington, 1910. On security regulation, pp. 611-42; 669-75; 803-22; 1142-52; 1171-77; 1279-84.
    Hearings on the Bill H. R. 12811. Investigation and Report of Property Values, Together with the Status and Control of Stocks and Bonds of Carriers Subject to the Act to Regulate Commerce. February 15 and 16, 1912. [The "Physical Valuation Bill"]. Washington, 1912.
    .... *Amendment of Act to Regulate Commerce.* House Rep. 637, 63d Cong., 2nd Sess. Washington, 1914.

Proposed Amendments to Section 20 of the Act to Regulate Commerce ... House Rep. 681, 63d Cong., 2d Sess. Washington, 1914.

"Regulation of the Issuance of Stocks and Bonds by Common Carriers." Hearings before the Committee . . . *February 9 to March 17, 1914.* Washington, 1914.

Return of Railroads to Private Ownership. Hearings . . . 3 vols. Washington, 1919. On security regulation see Index, vol. iii, *s. v.* "Capitalization" and "Securities."

United States. Congress. Joint Committee on Interstate and Foreign Commerce. [The "Newlands Committee"]. *Hearings* . . . *Pursuant to Public J. Res. 25, a Joint Resolution Creating a Joint Sub-Committee* . . . *to Investigate the Conditions Relating to Interstate and Foreign Commerce, and the Necessity of Further Legislation Relating Thereto* ... 3 vols. Washington, 1916-18.
    Contains several discussions of security regulation.

United States. Congress. Senate. Committee on Interstate Commerce. *Valuation of the Several Classes of Property of Common Carriers. Report of the Committee* . . . *with Hearings.* Sen. Rep. 1290, 62d Cong., 3d Sess. Washington, 1913.
    Security regulation discussed.

Government Control and Operation of Railroads. Hearings before the Committee . . . *Pursuant to S. Res. 171* . . . Parts 1 to 7. Washington, 1918. On security regulation see Index, *s. v.* "Capitalization" and "Securities."

Extension of Tenure of Government Control of Railroads. Hearings ... 3 vols. Washington, 1919. On security regulation see Indexes, vols. i and iii, *s. v.* "Capitalization," "Securities," and "Stocks and Bonds."

United States. Railroad Securities Commission, *Report of the Railroad Securities Commission to the President and Letter of the President Transmitting the Report to Congress.* 62d Cong., 2d Sess. House Doc. no. 256. Washington, 1911.

——, *Indexes to Evidence.* Printed in small number at Government Printing Office.
    The evidence itself, amounting to about 5,000 typewritten pages, was not printed, but copies were supplied to each member of the Commission and to the Interstate Commerce Commission.

——, *References to State Laws in Regard to Securities of Railroad Corporations, Compiled January, 1911.* Washington, 1911.

Wang, Ching Chun, *Legislative Regulation of Railway Finance in England.* University of Illinois Studies in the Social Sciences, vol. vii, nos. 1-2. Urbana, 1918.

Warren, Bentley, "Regulation in Massachusetts. Discussion of the Report of the Railroad Securities Commission." *Aera,* vol. i (1913), pp. 672-77.

Whitten, Robert H., *Regulation of Public Service Companies in Great Britain; with Supplementary Chapters on the Boston Sliding Scale and Toronto Auction Sale and Maximum Dividend Plans.* New York, 1914. Reprint of Appendix G of the *Annual Report of the New York Public Service Commission for the First District, December 31, 1913.*

——, *Valuation of Public Service Corporations; Legal and Economic Phases of Valuation for Rate Making and Public Purchase.* 2 vols. New York, 1914. On problems of security issues see Index, *s. v.* " Capitalization."

Wickersham, George W., *Federal Control of Stock and Bond Issues by Interstate Carriers. An Address before the Illinois State Bar Association, Chicago, Illinois, June 24, 1910.* Washington, 1910. Reprinted in *The Changing Order; Essays on Government, Monopoly, and Education, Written during a Period of Readjustment.* New York, 1914.

Williams, Judge W. D., see Haney, Lewis H., ed.

Williams, William H., *Letter to the Railroad Securities Commission in Reply to Their Request for Information and Opinions upon Questions pertaining to the Issuance of Stocks and Bonds of American Railways.* New York, 1911.

Wyman, Bruce, see also Beale & Wyman.

——, *Wyman on Public Service Corporations.* Full title: *The Special Law Governing Public Service Corporations, and all Others Engaged in Public Employment.* 2 vols. New York, 1911. Vol. ii, ch. xxxii, topic B, " Outstanding Capitalization."

INDEX

A

Accounts, manipulation of, 22-24, 57-61; Alton case, 175, 183*f*.

Actual cost, capitalization as evidence of, 22-25; as basis of capitalization, 77-82, 98

Adams, C. F., Jr., evils of stock watering, 15 n. 3

Adams, J., Jr., shares without par, 100 n.

Adamson, Representative, railway securities bill, 30 n. 1

Allied Packers, Inc., shares without par, 105 n. 1

Alton (*see* Chicago & Alton)

Anthracite Coal Rate Case (I. C. C.), 161 n. 3

Arizona statutes, on purposes of issue, 79 n. 5; stock below par, 94

Assets, capitalization and (*see* Capitalization)

Atlantic Lobos Oil Co., shares without par, 105 n. 1

Atwood, A. W., shares without par, 100 n.

Auction, sale of stock at, 138

B

Babylon Electric Light Co., *Re* (N. Y. P. S. C. 2nd Dist.), 79 n. 3

Bachrach *v.* Consolidated Gas, *etc.* (Md. P. S. C.), 158 n. 1, 166

Balance Sheet (*see also* Accounts), entry of no-par shares, 118-20, 122 n. 3; Alton finance, 171, 183*f*.

Barron, M. L., 11; stock dividends, 74 n. 2; purposes of issue, 79 n. 5; stock below par, 94 n. 2; state laws on security regulation, 133 n. 1; principles of security regulation, 135; ratio of stocks to bonds, 141

Basis of Capitalization (*see* Contents of Ch. III), bibliography, 195]

64; the problem, 64-67; rate-making value as, 67-73, 88; original investment as, 74-77, 88, 98; actual cost as, 77-82, 88, 98; market value as, 82-88, 178*f*.; earning capacity as, 82-88, 178*f*.; conflicting practices of commissions, 88-91; summary, 98*f*.

Bauer, J., 12; control of rates by security issues, 138 n. 1; capitalization and fair value, 158 n. 2

Bay State Rate Case (Mass. P. S. C.), 89 n. 2

Beale & Wyman, rate of return, 31 n. 3; capitalization and fair value, 156 n. 1, 157

Ben Avon Borough *v.* Ohio Valley Co. (Pa. P. S. C.), 158 n. 2

Bennett, R. J., shares without par, 101

Bibliographies, relation of capitalization to rates, 14; basis of capitalization, 64; shares without par, 100*f*.; security regulation, 186-94

Black Stream Electric Co., Appl. of (Me. P. U. C.), 94 n. 3

Blackstone management of Alton, 170, 183

Bonds and other evidences of debt, excess more dangerous than watered stock, 45-48; overissues furthered by forbidding sale of stock below par, 94, 109; income bonds, 48*f*.; ratio to stock, 139-46; sale at discount by Alton, 170*f*., 175, 177

Bonus stock, criticized and defended, 53 n. 1

Book values (*see also* Capitalization), relation to capitalization, 22-25, 59-61

Borrowing (*see* Bonds and other evidences of debt)